THE WISDOM
of the
PROPHET

THE WISDOM
of the
PROPHET

Sayings of Muhammad

Thomas Cleary

SHAMBHALA
Boston & London
2001

SHAMBHALA PUBLICATIONS, INC.
Horticultural Hall
300 Massachusetts Avenue
Boston, Massachusetts 02115
www.shambhala.com

9 8 7 6 5 4 3 2 1

Printed in the United States of America

⊛ This edition is printed on acid-free paper the meets the
American National Standards Institute z39.48 Standard.
Distributed in the United States by Random House, Inc.,
and in Canada by Random House of Canada Ltd

LIBRARY OF CONGRESS CATALOGING-IN-PUBLICATION DATA
The Wisdom of the Prophet: sayings of Muhammad/
translated from the Arabic by Thomas Cleary.
p. cm.
Two hundred and twenty-four authentic Ḥadīth chiefly
taken from Bukhārī's authoritative Ṣaḥīḥ, a few from
Nawawī's popular Riyāḍ al-ṣāliḥīn.
ISBN 1-57062-825-4 (alk. paper)
1. Hadith—Texts. I. Cleary, Thomas F., 1949–
II. Bukhārī, Muḥammad ibn Ismāʿīl, 810–870.
Jāmiʿ al-ṣaḥīḥ. English. Selections. III. Series.
BP135.A3W57   1994   94-6188
297'.1240521—dc20   CIP

TRANSLATOR'S INTRODUCTION

Mᴜʜᴀᴍᴍᴀᴅ ᴛʜᴇ Pʀᴏᴘʜᴇᴛ lived from 570 to 632 ᴄᴇ. A direct descendant of Abraham, the "Friend of God," through his son Ishmael, the ancestor of the Arabic people, Muḥammad was born to a family of the Quraish, the noblest tribe of Arabia. The Quraish were the hereditary custodians of the Ka'ba, the ancient Cube shrine in Mecca believed to have originally been built by Abraham himself.

The lifetime of Muḥammad was an era of momentous events throughout the ancient world. China was unified for the first time in centuries, establishing the foundation for the magnificent Tang dynasty. Under Tang Chinese tutelage, Korea was also unified under the powerful Silla kingdom, the new nations of Tibet and Nanchao were founded by ancient peoples in Central Asia, and the first constitution of Japan was promulgated. In India, the great Buddhist king Harsha briefly revived the Gupta empire, while to the west, the Persian empire extended its conquests all the way to Egypt and Asia Minor. Persia was thus also embroiled in conflict with the Byzantine empire, which was itself wrenched by internal unrest and revolt.

Even though Muḥammad was born to a noble house, he was an orphan and grew up in poverty. In his early years he

worked as a shepherd, then later joined the merchant caravans to greater Syria. He was married at the age of twenty-
five to a lady named Khadīja. Muḥammad had managed
some commercial affairs for Khadīja, and it was she who
proposed marriage, through the appropriate social chan-
nels, because of her admiration for his honesty and noble
character.

Muḥammad hesitated to marry Khadīja at first because
of his own lack of material means. Eventually the union did
take place, and Khadīja remained Muḥammad's only wife
for the rest of her life. She bore him a daughter, Fāṭima,
who later married ʿAlī, the Lion of God, one of the Prophet's earliest and most valiant companions.

Muḥammad's call to prophecy did not come until he was
forty years old, already a mature man with a distinguished
reputation in the community. Popularly known by the epi-
thets The True and The Trustworthy, Muḥammad was not
only an exemplary member of society, but also a profoundly
spiritual individual who regularly took to contemplative retreat in a mountain cave outside the city.

It was during such a retreat that revelation first came to
him, through the archangel Gabriel, who embraced the
Prophet in a powerful grip and told him, "Recite! Recite in
the name of your Lord, Who created: Who created humankind from a clot of blood. Recite, for your Lord is most
generous, Who taught by the Pen, taught humankind what
it did not know" (96:1–5).

Far from becoming inflated by such an experience, Muḥammad doubted himself. Rushing back to his wife, he told her he feared he was going mad, or else becoming a poet. She brought the Prophet to a cousin of hers, who was a Christian. This man confirmed that the revelation vouchsafed to Muḥammad was from the same source as the messages conveyed by Moses and Jesus. He also assured Muḥammad that as a prophet he would be opposed and ostracized when he made the revelation public, as had indeed happened to so many prophets in history.

As revelations progressed, the magnetism of the message drew people to the new religion of al-Islām, "Surrender to the Will of God." While one of the subsequent historical effects of Islam was to reunite the long-isolated Arabic people with the rest of the world, the original Islamic community surrounding Muḥammad already included people of African, Byzantine, and Persian origins as well as native Arabs. The new community accepted people of all classes, free or slave, uniting them in a common belief in the oneness of reality.

For the first three years, the teaching had been carried out in private, but eventually Muḥammad was instructed to take the message public. As had been predicted by the Christian Arab who originally recognized the message as Prophetic, for many years Muḥammad and the other Muslims were severely persecuted, until they finally emigrated from Mecca to Medina.

The Muslims fought back against oppression, outnumbered and outgunned though they were. Eventually, after inflicting many indignities and hardships on the Muslims, the opposition gave up, unable to break the will of the growing community of believers. Ten years after his emigration, shortly before his death, Muḥammad led a group of tens of thousands of pilgrims peacefully into Mecca for the greater pilgrimage (al-ḥajj).

Muḥammad viewed the religion of Islam as the completion of the Prophetic tradition beginning with Adam and continued by Noah, Abraham, Moses, and Jesus. This idea is expounded both in the Qur'ān, the revealed Book of Islam, and in the Ḥadīth, or traditional accounts of the Prophet's sayings and actions.

The Qur'ān and the Ḥadīth are the two main literary sources for Islam. Naturally, the Qur'ān is considered preeminent as a revelation from God. The Ḥadīth also include some extra-Qur'anic revelations from God (in the "Sacred Ḥadīth") but mostly recount the words and deeds of the Prophet himself, which are called the "Noble Ḥadīth." The Ḥadīth is the basis of Sunna, or Prophetic Custom, which clarifies the teaching of the Qur'ān in practical matters of inward and outward conduct.

This volume presents two hundred and twenty-four authentic accounts of the Prophet Muḥammad, revealing both his profound worldly wisdom and his lofty spiritual vision. Most of the selections are taken from Bukhariy's authoritative Ṣaḥīḥ, a few from Nawawī's popular Riyāḍ al-Ṣāliḥīn. I have departed from the traditional method of arrangement of these sources, however, which groups accounts in categories to facilitate scholarly research. To avoid blunting the palate of the ordinary reader by this approach, I have "scattered" the accounts to provide a variety of intermingled impressions, adding my own title to each anecdote to accent a salient image or idea.

Authentic accounts of the Prophet reveal him as a pragmatic man, down to earth yet brilliantly spiritual, stern in matters of right yet compassionate and clement, rich in dignity yet extremely modest and humble; a poignant storyteller gifted with a keen sense of humor, a manly and valorous warrior who was most kind and gentle with women and children; a diligent worker, a conscientious family man, a good neighbor, a just king.

THE WISDOM
of the
PROPHET

The Word of Wisdom

THE PROPHET said, "The word of wisdom is the stray of the believer, who has the better right to it wherever it may be found."

Learning

THE PROPHET said, "Seeking knowledge is incumbent upon every Muslim."

The Prophet also said, "Whoever goes out in search of knowledge is on the Path of God until returning."

Teaching

THE PROPHET said, "Return to your people and teach them."

The Prophet also said, "Let the one who is present impart knowledge to the one who is absent."

The women said to him, "The men have more access to you than do we; so please appoint a day for us to have access to you." So the Prophet set a day on which he met with the women and gave them advice and direction.

Writing

THE PROPHET told Zaid ibn Thābit to learn the writing of the Jews, so he came to write the Prophet's letters for him, and he read their letters when they wrote to the Prophet.

One of the Helpers* came to the Prophet and said, "O Messenger of God, I hear a saying from you that pleases me, but I cannot remember it."

The Prophet said, "Seek help from your right hand." And he mimed the act of writing.

God Is Peace

ᶜABDULLĀH said, "When we prayed behind the Prophet, may God bless him and grant him peace, we used to say, 'Peace upon Gabriel and Michael, peace upon so-and-so.'

"Then the Prophet turned to us and said, 'In fact, God *is* peace. So when any one of you prays, then say, "All benedictions are for God; and so are all prayers and all that is good. Peace upon you, O Prophet, and the mercy and blessing of God. Peace upon us, and upon all genuine servants of God," for if you say this, it will reach out to every true servant of God in the heavens and the earth; "I testify

---

*The "Helpers" were Muslim citizens of Medina who formed special bonds of fellowship with the Emigrant Muslim families to help the nascent community of Islam survive its early trials.

that there is nothing worthy of worship but God and that Muḥammad is a servant and messenger of God." ' "

Debt and Dishonesty

ᶜĀʾISHA, wife of the Prophet, related that he used to call to God in prayer, "O God, I take refuge with You from the torment of the grave, and I take refuge with You from the temptation of the false messiah. I take refuge with you from the trial of life and the trial of death. O God, I take refuge with You from sin and debt."

Someone asked the Prophet why he frequently sought refuge with God from debt. The Prophet replied, "When a man is in debt, he lies when he speaks and breaks promises he has made."

The Fear of the Prophet

THE PROPHET went out one day and prayed for the martyrs of the battle of Uhud. Then he went to the pulpit and said, "I am your vanguard, and I am your witness. And I, by God, I see my resource even now; and I have been given the keys of the treasuries of earth. And by God, I do not fear for you that you will associate partners with God after my passing, but I fear for you that you will compete with each other here on earth."

Prophetic Custom

IT IS RELATED that the Prophet used to say, at the end of every prayer, "There is nothing worthy of worship but God, Who is One and has no partner. To God belongs dominion; to God belongs all praise; and God is in control of everything. O God! No one can withhold what You have granted, and no one can grant what You have withheld. And the luck of the lucky does not avail them but for You."

It is also written of the Prophet that he used to forbid idle rumor and gossip, excessive questioning, and the squandering of wealth. He also forbade insolence to mothers, and burying daughters alive, and stinginess and importunity.

Dreams and Lies

THE PROPHET said, "The falsest of lies is to claim to have had a dream that one has not had."

Good Dreams and Bad

THE PROPHET said, "A good dream is from God. So if any of you have a dream of what you love, do not speak of it except to someone you love. And if any of you has a dream of what you dislike, then seek refuge in God from its evil, and from the evil of obsession; and spit thrice and do not tell anyone of it, for in fact it will not harm you."

An Invocation

ABŪ BAKR asked the Prophet to teach him an invocation to invoke in his prayers. The Prophet told him to say, "O God, I have oppressed my own soul greatly, and no one forgives sins but You, so please forgive me with forgiveness from You, and have mercy on me; for You are the epitome of forgiveness and mercy."

A Soul

A FUNERAL PROCESSION passed in front of the Prophet, and he stood up. Then he was told it was the bier of a Jew. The Prophet said, "Is it not a soul?"

On the Way to the Grave

THE PROPHET said, "When a corpse is placed in the coffin, and the men take it upon their shoulders, if it was a righteous person, it will say, 'Send me off!' If it was not a good person, it will say, 'Woe to it! Where are they taking it?' Everything will hear its voice, except humankind; for if a human being heard it, he would be stupefied."

Funerals

THE PROPHET said, "Be prompt with funerals, because if the deceased were righteous, then you are sending them on to good; and if they were bad, then you are getting evil off your necks."

Salvation

A JEWISH BOY who used to serve the Prophet fell ill, so the Prophet went to visit him. Sitting near the boy's pillow, the Prophet said to him, "Surrender to God."

The boy looked to his father, who was also there. The man told his son to obey Muḥammad, so he surrendered to God.

Then the Prophet came out and said, "Praise be to God, Who saved him from the Fire!"

Nature and Conditioning

THE PROPHET said, "No one is born except according to intrinsic nature, but their parents make them Jews, or Christians, or Magians, just as a cow gives birth to a calf that is whole; do you find it mutilated?"

Then Abū Huraira said, quoting the Qur'ān, "The intrinsic nature from God is that according to which God made humankind. There is no changing the creation of God; that is the true religion."

The Reward of Charity

THE PROPHET said, "If someone gives as charity so much as the equivalent of a single date from honest earnings—and God accepts only what is honest—God takes it in the Right Hand, then makes it increase for the one responsible, just as one of you raises a foal, until it becomes as big as a mountain."

A Threefold Reward

THE PROPHET said, "When a woman gives of the food in her home without causing ruin or trouble, she has her reward for what she gave, and her husband has his reward for having earned it; and the shopkeeper has a similar reward. The reward of one does not decrease the reward of the others at all."

A Word of Charity

TWO MEN came to the Prophet, one complaining of poverty, the other complaining of highway robbery.

The Prophet said, "As far as highway robbery is concerned, in fact it will be but a while before a caravan may go out to Mecca without a guard.

"And as for poverty, in fact the Hour will not be established until one of you wanders around with his gift of charity, not finding anyone to take it from him.

"Then each one of you will most surely stand before God, with no veil between you and God, and no interpreter to interpret for you.

"Then God will most surely say, 'Did I not give you wealth?'

"And you will say, 'Yes!'

"Then God will surely say, 'Did I not send a Messenger to you?'

"And you will say, 'Yes!' And you will look to your right and see nothing but Fire; and you will look to your left and see nothing but Fire.

"So each of you should ward off the Fire from yourself, even by half a date given in charity; or if you cannot find that, then by a good word."

Hidden Design

THE PROPHET related, "A man said, 'I will give a gift of charity,' and he went out with his gift and placed it in the hand of a thief.

"The next morning, people were saying the gift had been made to a thief. So the man said, 'O God, all praise belongs to You! I will give another gift of charity!' And he went out with his gift and placed it in the hand of a whore.

"The next morning, they were saying the gift had been given to a whore the night before. So the man said, 'O God, all praise belongs to You! She to whom I gave the gift was a whore. I will give another gift of charity.' And he went out with his gift and placed it in the hand of a rich man.

"The next morning, they were saying the gift had been made to a rich person. So the charitable man said, 'O God, all praise belongs to You! I gave alms to a thief, a whore, and a rich man!'

"Then someone came and said to him, 'As for your gift to the thief, it might get him to refrain from stealing out of embarrassment. As for the whore, it might get her to refrain from whoring out of embarrassment. As for the rich man, he might take a lesson from it and give of what God has bestowed on him.' "

The Obligation of Charity

THE PROPHET said, "Charity is incumbent upon every Muslim."

The people asked him, "O Prophet of God, what about one who has nothing to give?"

The Prophet said, "Then one works with one's own hands to support oneself and to give to others."

They asked, "And if one cannot find work?"

The Prophet said, "Then one should be good and refrain from evil; for that in fact is charity for the one who does so."

The Greatest Gift

Some people from the Helpers asked of the Prophet, and he gave to them. Then they asked again, and he gave again. Then they kept asking, until everything the Prophet had was gone.

Now the Prophet said, "I have no goods, nor would I keep any from you. And whoever tries to be modest, God will make modest; and whoever tries to be patient, God will make patient. And no one is given a gift that is better or greater than patience."

Moderation

Once the Prophet went into the mosque and saw a rope stretched between two pillars. He said, "What is this rope?"

They said, "This rope is Zainab's. When she weakens from fatigue, she hangs on to it."

The Prophet said, "No! Untie it! Let each of you pray to the extent of your energy, then sit down when you are tired."

Injunctions

The Prophet said, "Free captives, accept invitations."

Freeing Slaves

THE PROPHET said, "Whoever manumits his share of a jointly owned slave should free the slave completely if he has the money; otherwise, let him find gainful employment for the slave, without overworking him."

Charity and Family Support

ZAINAB, wife of 'Abdullāh, was in the mosque and saw the Prophet telling women to give charity, even of their jewelry.

As it happened, Zainab was supporting 'Abdullāh and a number of orphans in her charge. So now she told 'Abdullāh to go ask the Prophet whether it would do for her to support 'Abdullāh and the orphans in her charge as part of charity. 'Abdullāh told her to go ask him herself.

So Zainab went to the Prophet. At the Prophet's door, she found a woman from the Helpers who had the same concern as Zainab herself.

Now Bilāl passed by, and the two women asked him to ask the Prophet for them whether it would do for a woman to support her husband and orphans in her charge as part of charity. And they enjoined Bilāl not to inform the Prophet about them.

So Bilāl went in and presented the question. The Prophet asked him who the two women were, and Bilāl mentioned Zainab's name. The Prophet asked, "Which Zainab?" Bilāl replied that it was the wife of 'Abdullāh.

The Prophet said, "The answer is yes, and she will have two rewards: reward for taking care of relatives, and reward for charity."

Possessiveness and Liberality

Someone asked of the Prophet three times, and the Prophet gave him something each time. Then the Prophet said, "This resource is a fresh sweet fruit, and whoever takes it in a spirit free from possessiveness is blessed in it, while whoever takes it in a possessive spirit is not blessed in it, and is one who eats but is not sated. It is better to give than to receive."

Modesty

'Umar related, "The Messenger of God, may God bless him and grant him peace, used to give me gifts, but I said, 'Give it to someone who is poorer than I am.'

"The Prophet said, 'Take it. When something from this resource comes to you, and you are not possessive or importunate, then take it. Otherwise, do not let yourself pursue it.'"

Self-Reliance

THE PROPHET said, "If one of you takes a rope and gets up early to go into the mountains and cut firewood, sells it, and eats from this and gives charity from it, that is better for you than to ask of others."

Good and Bad Companions

THE PROPHET said, "Good companions and bad companions are like sellers of musk and the furnace of the smithy. You lose nothing from the musk seller, whether you buy some or smell or are imbued with its fragrance. The furnace of the smithy, on the other hand, burns your house and your clothes, or you get a noxious odor."

Expiation

A MAN came to the Prophet and said, "I am ruined!"

The Prophet asked, "What is the matter?"

The man said, "I had sexual intercourse with my wife while I was fasting."

The Prophet asked, "Do you have a slave to free?"

The man said, "No."

The Prophet asked, "Then can you fast for two successive months?"

The man said, "No."

The Prophet then asked, "Do you have the means to feed sixty paupers?"

The man said, "No."

Then the Prophet stopped. During the ensuing silence, a basket of dates was brought to the Prophet, who said, "Where is the inquirer?"

The man responded, "Here I am."

The Prophet said, "Take this and give it in charity."

But the man said, "Shall I give it to someone poorer than I am, O Messenger of God? For I swear by God, there is no family in this area that is poorer than mine."

The Prophet smiled broadly and said, "Feed your family with it."

Rights

THE PROPHET said to 'Abdullāh, "Have I not been informed that you fast all day and stand in prayer all night?"

'Abdullāh replied, "Yes, O Messenger of God!"

The Prophet said, "Don't do that. Fast, then eat and drink; stand in prayer, then sleep. For your body has a right over you, and your wife has a right over you; and your guest has a right over you. In fact, it is enough for you to fast three days of every month; indeed, since every good act is ten times its like to your credit, that is equivalent to fasting all the time."

Family Ties

THE PROPHET said, "Whoever would be glad to have his livelihood expanded and his life prolonged should maintain family ties."

Work

THE PROPHET said, "No one eats better food than that earned by the work of his own hands. Indeed, God's prophet David, peace be upon him, used to eat from the labor of his own hands."

The Prophet also said, "David, in fact, peace be upon him, never ate but from the work of his own hands."

The Witness

ʿATĀʾ IBN YASAR said to ʿAbdullāh ibn ʿAmr ibn al-ʿĀṣ, "Tell me of the description of the Prophet of God, may God bless him and grant him peace, that is in the Torah."

ʿAbdullāh said, "Certainly! For by God, he is described in the Torah, with some of the description that is in the Qurʾān." And he recited:

O Prophet,
We have sent you as a witness,
and a bearer of good news,
and a warner,

and a refuge for the unlettered.
You are My servant, and My messenger;
I name you the One Who Trusts in God,
who is not uncivil, and not inconsiderate,
not a noisemaker in the markets.
He does not rebut evil by evil,
but pardons and forgives.
And God will not have him die
until he sets the crooked community straight,
so that they say
there is no divinity but God,
by which will be opened
blind eyes, deaf ears, and closed minds.

Everyday Ethics

THE PROPHET forbade a town dweller to broker for a
nomad; he forbade anyone to bid up a price to jack it up
artificially; he forbade anyone to sell anything so as to nul-
lify a previous sale by another; he forbade anyone to try to
buy something already sold to another; he forbade a man to
propose marriage to another's fiancée; and he forbade
women to seek the divorce of other women in order to take
their places.

Adversaries of God

THE PROPHET said, "God has said, 'I will be the adversary of three types of people on the Day of Resurrection: those who offer in My name but then betray their promise; those who sell a free individual and consume the price obtained; and those who hire workers and have work done but do not give them their wages.' "

The Plea of the Oppressed

THE PROPHET sent Muʿādh to the Yemen, saying, "Beware the plea of the oppressed, for there is no screen between it and God."

Scales of Justice

THE PROPHET said, "Whoever is guilty of injustice against a fellow human being, whether in regard to his honor or anything else, let him seek his pardon for the Day of Resurrection, before there is no money. If he has any good works to his credit, they will be taken from him to the extent of his injustice. And if he has no good deeds to his credit, the sins of the other will be taken and loaded on him."

Human Error

WHEN THE Prophet heard an argument at the door of his apartment, he went out and addressed the disputers, saying, "I am only a human being, but antagonists in disputes come to me; and it may happen that one of you is more eloquent than another, and I may consider him right and judge in his favor because of that. So if I give the right of a Muslim to another, that is a bit of Hellfire, which he may take or leave."

A Harvest of Charity

THE PROPHET said, "If any Muslim plants a tree or sows a crop, and then a bird, a human being, or an animal eats of it, then it is sacred charity to his credit."

Every Living Being

THE PROPHET related, "While a man was walking, he became extremely thirsty, so he went down into a well and drank from it. Then he came out, only to find a panting dog eating moist earth in its thirst. The man said, 'The same thing has happened to this creature as happened to me.' So he filled his shoe, climbed out holding it in his teeth, and thus gave the dog water to drink. Then God thanked the man and forgave him."

People asked, "O Messenger of God, are we rewarded for our treatment of animals?"

The Prophet said, "There is a reward for your treatment of every living thing."

Brotherhood

THE PROPHET said, "A Muslim is brother to a Muslim; let one not oppress another or betray him. And whoever sees to the need of his brother, God sees to his need. And whoever relieves a Muslim from distress will be relieved by God from distress on the Day of Resurrection. And whoever protects a Muslim will be protected by God on the Day of Resurrection."

Jesus and God

THE PROPHET said, "Jesus saw a man stealing and said to him, 'Did you steal?' The man said, 'No, by God, Who alone is worthy of worship.' Jesus said, 'I believe in God and suspect my eyes.'"

Islam versus "Mohamedanism"

THE PROPHET said, "Do not lavish praise on me as the Christians have lavished praise on the son of Mary; for I am only a slave. So call me God's slave and messenger."

Unequal Justice

THE PROPHET said, "What destroyed those before you was that whenever an aristocrat among them stole, they would let him be, but when one of the powerless among them stole, they would inflict the legal punishment on him."

Forgiveness

THE PROPHET said, "There was a man who lent money to people. He used to say to his servant, 'When you give to someone who is poor, be forgiving, that God may be forgiving to us.' And that man met God, and God pardoned him."

Paradise and Hellfire

THE PROPHET said, "Paradise and Hellfire had an argument. Hellfire said, 'I have been favored with the imperious and the proud.'

"Paradise said, 'What is the matter with me, that none enter me but the powerless and lowly people?'

"God said to Paradise, 'You are My mercy; you are the instrument of My compassion upon any of My servants that I will.'

"And God said to Hellfire, 'You are only the punishment

by which I punish any of My servants that I will. And both of you shall have your fill.'

"As for Hellfire, it will not be filled until God steps on it and calls a halt; then it will be full, and its parts will be contracted toward one another. And God will not be unjust to a single member of Creation.

"And as for Paradise, God will bring into a being a new Creation for it."

Mercy and Wrath

THE PROPHET said, "On completing the Creation, God wrote in the Book of God, which is with God on the Throne, 'My Mercy prevails over My wrath.' "

The Son of Adam

THE PROPHET said, "God Most High said, 'The son of Adam scorns Me, and it is not right for him to scorn Me. And he disbelieves Me, and it is not right for him to disbelieve Me. As for his scorn, he says I have a son. And as for his disbelief in Me, he says God will not re-create him as God created him to start with.' "

Paradise

THE PROPHET said, "The minutest place in the Garden is better than this world and everything in it."

Hypocrisy

THE PROPHET said, "A certain man will be brought to the Fire on the Day of Resurrection; he will be thrown into the Fire, so that his guts spill out into the Fire; and he will go round and round like a donkey at a mill. The inhabitants of Hellfire will gather around him and say, 'Hey, you! What is the matter with you? Did you not used to enjoin us to be good and forbid us from evil?' He will say, 'I used to enjoin you to good, but did not do good myself; and I used to forbid you to do evil, but I did evil myself.' "

Humanity and Inhumanity

THE PROPHET said, "A woman entered Hellfire because of a cat that she kept tied up, neither feeding it nor letting it go to eat of the vermin of the earth."

He also related, "One of the prophets stopped to rest under a tree, and an ant stung him. The prophet had his baggage removed from beneath the tree and ordered that fire be set to the ants' abode. But then God inspired him with the thought, 'Why not just one ant?' "

The Prophet also narrated, "A prostitute was forgiven because she passed by a dog panting at a well, and, observing that thirst was about to kill the dog, she removed her slipper, fastened it to her veil, and drew out some water for the dog. And so she was forgiven because of that."

Taking Heed

THE PROPHET said, "Do not enter the dwelling places of those who wronged themselves unless you do so weeping, lest the same thing happen to you as happened to them."

Fasting and Prayer

THE PROPHET said, "The fast most loved by God is the fast of David, who would fast for one day and break his fast for one day. And the prayer most loved by God is the prayer of David, who would sleep half the night, then get up and pray for a third of the night, then sleep for a sixth of the night."

Admission to Paradise

THE PROPHET said, "Whoever testifies that there is no god but God, the One, with no partner, and that Muḥammad is a servant and messenger of God, and that Jesus is a servant and messenger of God, a word from God bestowed on Mary, a spirit from God, and that Paradise is true and Hell is true, will be admitted by God into Paradise whatever works he has done."

Jesus and Muḥammad

THE PROPHET said, "I am the closest of all people to Jesus, son of Mary, in this world and the Hereafter; for all prophets are brothers, with different mothers but one religion."

Moses and Muḥammad

TWO MEN were railing at each other. One was a Muslim, the other a Jew.

The Muslim said, "By God, Who has chosen Muḥammad in preference to all beings!"

The Jew said, "By God, Who has chosen Moses in preference to all beings!"

Now the Muslim raised his hand at that and slapped the Jew in the face. So the Jew went to the Prophet and informed him about what had happened between him and the Muslim.

The Prophet called the Muslim to him and asked him what had happened. The Muslim told him.

The Prophet said, "Do not consider me better than Moses, for all humankind will be struck unconscious on the Day of Resurrection, and I will be struck unconscious with them. Now, I will be the first to regain consciousness, but when I do, there will be Moses by the side of the Throne. I do not know if he will have been one of those struck unconscious and will have awakened before me, or if he will have been one exempted by God."

Reneging on Gifts

THE PROPHET said, "One who takes back his gift is like a dog that eats up its own vomit."

Give Ungrudgingly

THE PROPHET said, "Give ungrudgingly, lest God be grudging toward you; and do not withhold, lest God withhold from you."

Gifts and Bribes

'UMAR IBN 'ABDUL AZĪZ said, "In the lifetime of the Prophet, may God bless him and grant him peace, a gift was a gift. Today, it is a bribe."

Reconciliation

THE PROPHET said, "One who reconciles people by attributing good or saying something good is not a liar."

The Greatest Right

THE PROPHET said, "The conditions that have the greatest right to be completely fulfilled are those which make the private parts of women legal to you."

Charity

THE PROPHET said, "There is charity incumbent upon every bone of a human being on every day that the sun rises. To judge fairly between two people is charity. To help someone mount or load his pack animal is charity. A good word is charity. Every step on the way to prayer is charity. Removal of what is harmful from the road is charity."

Nearby

ABŪ MŪSĀ AL-ASHʿARĪ related, "We were with the Messenger of God, may God bless him and grant him peace, and whenever we climbed up to high ground, we would declare the uniqueness and majesty of God, and our voices would rise. So the Prophet said, 'O people, steady yourselves! You are not calling someone who is deaf or absent; for God is with you, all-hearing, nearby.'"

Travel

THE PROPHET said, "Travel is a piece of torment, interfering with your sleeping and eating and drinking. So when you have concluded your business, hasten to your family."

Names for God

THE PROPHET said, "There are ninety-nine names for God, one hundred minus one; whoever knows them will enter Paradise."

An Endowment

'UMAR acquired some land in Khaibar, and he went to the Prophet to seek counsel in regard to it. 'Umar said, "O Messenger of God, I have acquired some land in Khaibar, which is more valuable than any other property I have ever acquired. What would you have me do with it?"

The Prophet said, "If you wish, devote its assets to charity."

So 'Umar donated it for charity on the condition that it not be sold, given away, or inherited, and that it be used to give charity for the poor, for kinfolk, for freeing slaves, for the cause of God, for travelers, and for visitors. It was not a misdemeanor for the custodian to eat of it fairly, and to feed others, without capitalizing on it.

Last Will and Testament

THE PROPHET said, "A Muslim person who has anything to leave should not spend two nights without having a written will with him."

Treatment of Slaves

THE PROPHET said, "Slaves are your brothers, so feed them with what you yourselves eat."

The Prophet also said, "Your slaves are your brothers, whom God has placed under your control. So whoever has his brother under his control should feed him and clothe him with what he himself eats and wears; and do not assign him a task that is too much for him, or if you do, then help him."

The Prophet also said, "Whoever has a female slave and educates her, treats her well, then frees her and marries her, has a double reward."

Fighting

THE PROPHET said, "If any of you fight, avoid the face."

Gifts and Alms

WHENEVER FOOD was brought to the Prophet, he would ask if it was a gift or alms for charity. If he was told it was alms for charity, the Prophet would tell his companions to eat it, and would not partake of it himself. If he was told it was a gift, he would eat with them.

The Rights of the Streets

THE PROPHET said, "Beware of sitting in the streets."

People said, "We have no way to avoid it, for that is where we sit and talk."

The Prophet said, "Then when you sit there, give the street her rights."

They asked, "What are the rights of the street?"

The Prophet replied, "Lowering the gaze, refraining from causing trouble, returning greetings, enjoining good, and forbidding evil."

Usurpation of Land

THE PROPHET said, "Whoever seizes a piece of land unjustly will be sunk in the ground to the distance of seven earths on the Day of Resurrection."

The Second Coming of Christ

THE PROPHET said, "The Hour will not be established until the son of Mary descends into your midst as a just arbitrator, whereupon he will break the cross, kill the swine, and set aside the special tax on non-Muslim citizens of Muslim lands. And there will be so much money that no one will accept it."

The Debts of the Rich

THE PROPHET said, "It is unjust for a rich man to delay payment of his debts."

Purgatory

THE PROPHET said, "When the believers are clear of Hell-fire, they will be detained on a bridge between the Garden and the Fire, where they will avenge the wrongs between them in the world until they are cleansed and purified, when they will be allowed to enter the Garden. And by God, everyone will be in a dwelling in the Garden that is more appropriate than was their dwelling in the world."

Help

THE PROPHET said, "Help your brother, whether he be an oppressor or one of the oppressed."

Some said, "O Messenger of God, we help him if he is oppressed; but how can we help him if he is an oppressor?"

The Prophet said, "By stopping him."

Injustice

THE PROPHET said, "Injustice will be darkness on the Day of Resurrection."

Responsibilities

THE PROPHET said, "Every one of you is a caretaker and is responsible for his charge. So the leader is a caretaker and is responsible for his charge. A man is caretaker of his family and is responsible for his charge. A woman is caretaker of her husband's house and is responsible for her charge. A servant is caretaker of his employer's property and is responsible for his charge."

Disgrace

THE PROPHET said, "There are three kinds of people to whom God will not speak and whom God will not regard on the Day of Resurrection. One is a person who swears falsely of an item of commerce that he has been given more than he has actually been given. Another is a person who swears a false oath after the afternoon prayer in order to acquire thereby the property of a Muslim. The third is a person who withholds surplus water. And God will say, 'Today I withhold My grace from you, as you withheld the benefit of what you did not make yourself.' "

Generosity

THE PROPHET said, "If I had a mountain of gold, it would not please me if I still had any of it after three days, except something set aside for debts."

Settlement of Debts

ONCE THE PROPHET was sitting with a group of people when a funeral bier was brought to him with the request that the Prophet pray for the deceased.

The Prophet asked, "Was he in debt?"

They said, "No."

The Prophet asked, "Then did he leave anything?"

They said, "No."

So the Prophet prayed for the deceased.

Then another bier was brought with the request that the Prophet pray for the deceased.

The Prophet asked, "Was he in debt?"

"They said, "Yes."

The Prophet said, "And did he leave anything?"

They said, "Three dinars."

So the Prophet prayed for the deceased.

Then a third funeral bier was brought with the request that the Prophet pray for the deceased.

The Prophet asked, "Did he leave anything?"

They said, "No."

The Prophet asked, "Then was he in debt?"

They said, "Three dinars."

The Prophet said to them, "You pray for your companion."

Then Abū Qatāda said, "Pray for him, O Messenger of God, and I will assume responsibility for his debt."

So the Prophet prayed for the deceased.

The Most Odious of Men

ᶜĀʼISHA related that the Prophet said, "The most odious of men to God is the one who is most quarrelsome."

What Will Happen

ᶜĀʼISHA related that the Prophet said, "Do you reckon you will enter the Garden without there happening to you the likes of what happened to those who passed away before you?"

The Doubt of Abraham

THE PROPHET said, "We have more right to doubt than Abraham did when he said, 'Lord, show me how You quicken the dead.' God said, 'Do you not believe?' Abraham replied, 'Oh, yes! But it would reassure my heart.'"

Poverty

THE PROPHET said, "The one in poverty is not the one you send away with a date or two, or a morsel or two. The one in poverty is the one who refrains from calling attention to himself."

Victory

THE PROPHET said, "There is no flight after victory, but struggle and planning. And if others are hostile to you, turn away."

Service

THE PROPHET said, "God does not look at your bodies, or at your forms, but looks at your hearts and your works."

Fighting

THE PROPHET was asked, "Of men who fight aggressively, those who fight defensively, and those who fight aloof, which of these are on the way of God?"

The Prophet said, "He who fights so that the word of God should be most honored is he who is on the way of God."

Killing

THE PROPHET said, "If the devotion of two Muslims is in their swords, both the killer and the killed are in for the Fire."

Someone remarked, "O Messenger of God, this befits the killer, but what about the one killed?"

The Prophet said, "He was in fact trying to kill his companion."

Repentance

THE PROPHET said, "By God, I seek forgiveness of God, and turn to God in repentance, more than seventy times a day."

It is also related that the Prophet said, "O people, turn to God in repentance, and seek forgiveness of God. Indeed, I repent a hundred times a day."

The Hand of God

THE PROPHET said, "The hand of God is full, and the flow of disbursal day and night does not diminish that."

He also said, "Do you see what God has spent since the creation of the heavens and the earth? Even that has not diminished what is in the hand of God."

The Extent of God

ᶜABDULLĀH related that a Jew came to the Prophet and said, "O Muḥammad! God holds the heavens on a finger, and the two earths on a finger, and the mountains on a finger, and the trees on a finger, and all created things on a finger. Then God says, 'I am the King.'"

At this the Messenger of God smiled broadly. Then he recited this passage of the Qurʾān: "And they have not assessed the true extent of God" [39:67].

'Abdullāh added, "'The messenger of God smiled' in wonder and agreement."

Dreams and Prophecy

THE PROPHET said, "When the Time approaches, the dream of the believer can hardly be belied. And the dream of the believer is one of the forty-six parts of prophecy, which surely is never belied."

Muḥammad ibn Sīrīn added, "And it used to be said that dreams were of three kinds: the talk of the self, terrorization by obsession, or good news from God. And if any dream something they dislike, let them not tell anyone of it, but get up and say a prayer."

A Gubernatorial Mandate

WHEN THE PROPHET sent two representatives to govern the Yemen, he told them, "Bring ease, not hardship. Bring good news, not horror. And cooperate willingly with each other."

Evil Suggestion

ONCE THE PROPHET'S WIFE Ṣafiyya came to him [while he was at the mosque], and he left with her when she returned home. On the way, two men from among the Helpers happened to pass by them. The Prophet called to them and said, "It is only Ṣafiyya."

The two men said, "Glory be to God!"

The Prophet said, "Evil suggestion circulates in the human being like the circulation of blood."

The Best of Defenders

IBN ʿABBĀS related, "The saying 'God is sufficient for us, and the best of defenders' was uttered by Abraham, peace be upon him, when he was thrown into the fire; and by Muḥammad, may God bless him and grant him peace, when they said the people were mobbing against him, and that he should fear them. And it strengthened both of them in faith, and they said, 'God is sufficient for us, and the best of defenders.' "

The Miser's Fate

THE PROPHET said, "If someone is given wealth by God but does not pay the welfare tax, his wealth will be represented to him on the Day of Resurrection as a viper encircling him, striking him with two streams of poison. It will seize him by the jaws and will say, 'I am your wealth; I am your hoard.' "

Signs of a Hypocrite

THE PROPHET said, "There are three signs of a hypocrite: he lies when he speaks, he breaks promises, and he is unfaithful to a trust."

Who Is a Muslim?

THE PROPHET said, "A Muslim is one from whose tongue and whose hand all Muslims are safe; and a refugee is one who flees from what God has forbidden."

The Desire of a Believer

THE PROPHET said, "None of you is a believer until you like for others what you like for yourself."

Faith, Submission, and Goodness

ONE DAY the Prophet was sitting with some people when the archangel Gabriel came to him and said, "What is faith?"

The Prophet replied, "Faith is to believe in God, in God's angels, and in meeting God; and in the messengers of God; and in the Resurrection."

Gabriel said, "What is submission?"

The Prophet replied, "Submission is to serve God and not attribute any partners to God, and to pray regularly, and to pay the prescribed welfare tax, and to fast during the month of Ramadan."

Gabriel said, "What is goodness?"

The Prophet replied, "To worship God as if you actually see God; for if you do not see God, God certainly sees you."

Intention and Reward

THE PROPHET said, "All works depend on intention, so everyone gets what he intended. Thus the emigration of those whose emigration was for God and God's Prophet was for God and God's Prophet; and the emigration of those whose emigration was for worldly gain or for a woman to marry was for what they emigrated for."

The Hour

ONCE WHILE the Prophet was talking to people in a gathering, a nomad of the desert came to him and said, "When is the Hour?" But the Prophet went on talking.

Some of the people said that the Prophet had heard what the desert nomad had said, but it had offended him. Others maintained on the contrary that the Prophet had not heard.

When the Prophet finished his talk, he said, "Where is the one who was here asking about the Hour?"

The desert nomad spoke up: "Here I am, O Messenger of God."

The Prophet said, "When trustworthiness is allowed to perish, expect the Hour."

The desert nomad asked, "How will it be lost?"

The Prophet replied, "When authority rests on unsuitable people, expect the Hour."

The Curse of the Miser

THE PROPHET said, "Every single day the slaves of God pass, two angels come down. One says, 'O God, give every generous one recompense!' The other says, 'O God, give every miser ruination!'"

Finery and Nakedness

THE PROPHET'S WIFE Umm Salama related, "The Prophet, may God bless him and give him peace, woke up one night and said, 'Glory to God! What trials have been revealed tonight, what treasures have been revealed tonight! Who will awaken the women in their rooms? One who dresses up in this world may be naked in the Hereafter!'"

Quarrelsome Humanity

ᶜALĪ related that one night the Prophet came to him and his wife Fāṭima, who was the Prophet's daughter. The Prophet said to them, "Do you not pray?"

'Alī replied, "O Messenger of God, our souls are in the hand of God, so if God willed to get us up, then God would get us up."

When 'Alī said that, the Prophet left without responding to them at all; but 'Alī reported that he heard the Prophet slapping his thigh and saying, "But humankind is more quarrelsome than anything" [18:54].

Charity at Home

THE PROPHET said, "When a man spends money on his family as a good deed, then for him it is a sacred act of charity."

Earning the Favor of God

THE PROPHET said, "You will not spend anything seeking the favor of God without being rewarded for it, even what you provide for your wife."

Three Individuals

WHILE THE PROPHET was sitting in the mosque along with some people, three individuals approached. Two of them came up to the Prophet, while the third went away.

The former two stood still before the Prophet; then one saw an opening in the circle and sat there, while the other sat behind them all.

As for the third, he turned his back and went away.

When the Prophet had finished the session, he said, "Shall I tell you about those three individuals? The first one sought refuge in God, and God sheltered him. The second was ashamed and embarrassed before God, and God spared him. As for the third, he turned away, so God turned away from him."

Consideration

IBN MAS'ŪD said, "The Prophet, may God bless him and grant him peace, was considerate of us in respect to the times of his lectures, hating to weary us."

The Order of God

THE PROPHET said, "Those for whom God wishes good, God causes to understand religion. I am only a distributor; God is the giver. And this community will not cease to observe the order of God, and those who differ will not hurt it, until the order of God is completed."

The Report of the Angels

THE PROPHET said, "Angels come to you in succession, some by night and some by day; and they all assemble at the morning and afternoon prayers. Then those who passed the night with you ascend, and God asks them, though God knows better than they, 'How were my servants when you left them?' And they say, 'When we left them, they were praying; and when we came to them, they were praying.' "

Satan's Fart

THE PROPHET said, "When the call to prayer is exclaimed, Satan turns away, farting so loud as not to hear the call. Then, when the call is finished, Satan approaches, until the second call to prayer within the mosque, whereupon he turns away. Then, when the second call is finished, Satan approaches and intervenes between a person and his soul, telling him to remember things he had not had in mind, so as to divert the person from awareness of how much he has prayed."

Prayer in Congregation

THE PROPHET said, "The prayer of a person in congregation is twenty-five times better than one's prayer alone or in the market. The reason for this is that when one performs the ablution and does it perfectly, and then goes out to the mosque, going out for the sole purpose of prayer, then one is elevated in degree with every step one takes, and absolved of a sin with every step. And when one prays, the angels continue to pray for one as long as one is praying, saying, 'O God, bless this one! O God, have mercy on this one!' And each one of you is at prayer as long as you are waiting for the prayer."

Whom to Envy

THE PROPHET said, "No one should envy anyone but two people: someone to whom God has given wealth and who is thus empowered to spend it righteously; and someone to whom God has given wisdom and who judges by it and teaches it."

Moderation

SOMEONE SAID to the Prophet, "By God, I am only absent from morning prayer on account of so-and-so, because he prolongs it on us."

The Prophet said, "Some of you shy away from it, so whoever of you leads the people in prayer should be moderate, because among the people are those who are weak, those who are old, and those who are in need."

Abū Masʿūd noted, "Never did I see the Messenger of God, may God bless him and grant him peace, more wroth in a lecture than on that day."

Supplications of the Prophet

ʿĀʾISHA said, "The Prophet, may God bless him and grant him peace, frequently would say in his bowing and prostration, 'Glory to You, O God, our Lord; and praise be to You, O God, please forgive me.'

"He based this on the Qurʾān."

Modesty

ANAS, who had been the Prophet's servant as a boy, related, "A feast of bread and meat was given for the Prophet, may God bless him and grant him peace, on the occasion of his marriage to Zainab bint Jaḥsh; I was sent to invite people to the repast. So some people would come, eat, and leave, whereupon others came, ate, and left. So I invited people until I couldn't find anyone else to invite.

"Then I said, 'O Prophet of God, I find no one else to invite.' He said, 'Take away the food, which is for all of you.'

"But there remained in the house a group of three people conversing, so the Prophet left and went to 'Ā'isha's home and said, 'Peace upon you, O people of the house, and the mercy of God.' And 'Ā'isha responded, 'And upon you peace, and the mercy of God. How did you find your wife? May God bless you.'

"Then he went to the houses of all his other wives, and said to them the same things he had said to 'Ā'isha; and they said to him the same things 'Ā'isha had said to him.

"Then the Prophet returned, only to find that the party of three was still in the house conversing.

"The Prophet was extremely shy; so he went out, heading for 'Ā'isha's house. I don't remember whether I told him or whether he was told by someone else, that the people had left; anyway, he went back.

"Now, as soon as his foot stepped on the threshold of the

door on his way in, he lowered a blind between us, and the Verse of the Veil was revealed."

People of Paradise and Hell

THE PROPHET said, "Shall I tell you about the people of Paradise? They include every one of those who are powerless and slighted, yet who certainly fulfill any oath to God they make. Shall I tell you about the people of Hell? They include everyone who is violent, recalcitrant, and arrogant."

The Divine Rigor

THE PROPHET said, "When God reveals the divine rigor, all the believers, male and female, will prostrate themselves before it. But there will remain those who used to prostrate themselves in the world to be seen and heard of; and when they try to prostrate themselves, their backs will be reduced to a single vertebra."

Faith and Works

ONCE WHEN the Prophet was sitting with a group of people, he said, "Every one of you has a place assigned in Hellfire or Paradise."

The people said, "Should we then rely on this, O Messenger of God?"

The Prophet said, "No! Work! For everyone has his way facilitated." Then the Prophet recited, "The giving and conscientious who believe in what is best, God will ease into great ease. The avaricious and complacent who deny what is best, God will ease into great difficulty" [92:5–10].

Reciting the Qur'ān

THE PROPHET said, "One who recites the Qur'ān is like a citron, whose flavor is good and whose scent is good. One who does not recite the Qur'ān is like a date, whose flavor is good but which has no scent. An immoral person who recites the Qur'ān is like basil, whose scent is good but whose taste is bitter. And an immoral person who does not recite the Qur'ān is like the colocynth, whose taste is bitter and which has no scent."

Spend

THE PROPHET said, "God Most High has said, 'Spend, O child of Adam, and I will spend on you.' "

Women at the Mosque

THE PROPHET said, "If your wife asks permission to go to the mosque, do not forbid her."

Care of Widows

THE PROPHET said, "One who looks after the widowed and the poor is like the warrior who struggles in the way of God, or like one who prays all night and fasts all day."

Something Better

FĀṬIMA, daughter of the Prophet, came to him asking for a servant. The Prophet said, "Shall I tell you about something that is better for you than that? When you go to bed, say 'Glory to God' thirty-three times, say 'All thanks and praise belong to God' thirty-three times, and say 'God is Greatest' thirty-four times."

The Prophet at Home

SOMEONE asked 'Ā'isha what the Prophet used to do at home. She said, "He used to remain occupied working for his family, then would go out when he heard the call to prayer."

The Poverty of the Prophet

ANAS said, "The Prophet, may God bless him and grant him peace, never ate fine bread, nor a scalded roast, until he met God."

Economy

THE PROPHET said, "Food for two suffices three; and food for three suffices four."

Frugality

THE PROPHET said, "A believer eats in one gut, while a disbeliever or a hypocrite eats in seven guts."

Gratitude

WHEN THE PROPHET finished his meal, he would say, "Thanks be to God, who has sufficed us and quenched our thirst. There is no refusal or denial."

When the dining sheet was removed, the Prophet would say, "All praise and thanks belong to God, so much that is good and blessed therein; there is no refusing, no leaving, and no dispensing with You, our Lord."

Belief in Action

THE PROPHET said, "God Most High has said, 'If I test a slave of Mine by his two beloved things [eyes] and he is patient, I will replace them for him by the Garden of Paradise.' "

A Woman of the People of Paradise

IBN 'ABBĀS said, "Shall I show you a woman of the people of Paradise? This black lady came to the Prophet, may God bless him and grant him peace, and said, 'I have epileptic seizures, and I become unveiled. Please invoke God for me.'

"The Prophet said, 'If you wish, endure patiently and you will have Paradise; or if you wish, I will call on God to cure you.'

"She said, 'I will be patient, but call on God for me to see that I will not be exposed.'

"So the Prophet called on God for her."

Feeding the Cook

THE PROPHET said, "When your servant brings you your meal, if you do not invite him to sit with you, then at least have him take some of the food for himself, for he is the one who suffered the heat of the stove and took pains to prepare it."

Mercy

THE PROPHET forbade the tying down of an animal, domestic or otherwise, in order to kill it.

The Prophet cursed anyone who mutilates an animal while it is still alive.

Drinking

THE PROPHET said, "Whoever drinks wine in this world and does not turn away from it will be deprived of it in the Hereafter."

Disbelief in Action

THE PROPHET said, "An adulterer is not a believer when he is committing adultery, and a drinker is not a believer when he is drinking wine, and a thief is not a believer when he is thieving."

The Compassion of the Prophet

THE DAUGHTER of the Prophet sent a message to him, saying, "We think my daughter is dying, so please come see us."

The Prophet sent her his greetings and this message: "It is up to God what God takes and what God gives; and all things are finite in God's perspective. So let her endure patiently in anticipation of God's reward."

But his daughter sent him another message, adjuring him to come. So the Prophet rose.

The child was placed in the Prophet's lap, her breath rattling, and the Prophet's eyes overflowed with tears.

"What is this, O Messenger of God?" asked Sa'd, one of the companions.

The Prophet said, "This is the compassion placed by God in the hearts of those of God's slaves whom God wishes to be compassionate. And God does not show compassion to any of God's slaves except the compassionate ones."

Have It Your Way

THE PROPHET went to see a sick bedouin. Now, whenever the Prophet visited someone who was ill, he would say, "Do not be troubled; it is a purification, God willing."

But the bedouin said, "Purification? Ha! It is just a fever boiling and raging against an old man, sending him to the grave."

The Prophet said, "Very well, then."

Suicide

THE PROPHET said, "Let none of you wish for death because of any loss or harm that has befallen you. But if you cannot avoid doing so, then say, 'O God, keep me alive as long as life is better for me, and take me if death is better for me.' "

Works and Grace

THE PROPHET said, "No one's works will get him into the Garden of Paradise."

Some of his companions rejoined, "Not even you, O Messenger of God?"

The Prophet said, "Not even me, unless God protects me with mercy and grace. So confine yourself to what is appropriate and fitting. And let no one wish for death, for if one is virtuous, one may increase in goodness, and if one is wicked, one may apologize to God."

The Healer

WHENEVER THE PROPHET visited someone who was ailing, or someone ill was brought to him, the Prophet would invoke blessings and peace upon the patient and say, "Take away the ill and heal, O God, for You are the Healer. There is no cure but Your cure, a cure that leaves no sickness."

Disease and Remedy

THE PROPHET said, "God has not sent down any disease without having sent down a remedy for it."

Black Nigella

THE PROPHET said, "There is a remedy in black nigella for every malady but death."

Two Mortal Sins

THE PROPHET said, "Avoid the two mortal sins: idolatry and witchcraft."

Family Ties

THE PROPHET said, "One who cuts off family ties does not enter the Garden of Paradise."

Good Relations

THE PROPHET said, " 'The Merciful' is a derivative of 'The Compassionate,' for God Most High has said, 'I will keep good relations with whoever keeps good relations with you; and I will cut off relations with anyone who cuts off relations with you.' "

Mercy

THE PROPHET said, "God rendered Mercy into a hundred parts, keeping ninety-nine parts and sending one part down to earth. By virtue of that one portion, creatures are merciful to one another, such that even the mare lifts her hooves away from her foal, fearing she may step on it."

The Prophet also said, "Whoever is not merciful will not be shown mercy."

Concern for Neighbors

THE PROPHET said, "Gabriel kept charging me with concern for neighbors, such that I thought he would have me appoint them my heirs."

Shielded from Hellfire

A WOMAN came to 'Ā'isha, wife of the Prophet, with two daughters. She asked for something, but found 'Ā'isha with nothing in her possession but a single date. 'Ā'isha gave her the date, and she divided it between her daughters. Then they left.

When the Prophet returned, 'Ā'isha told him about this incident. He remarked, "Whoever is responsible for these daughters in anything and treats them well will be shielded by them from hellfire."

A Single Body

THE PROPHET said, "You see the believers in their mutual kindness, love, and sympathy, as if they were a single body; when one of its members is ailing, the rest of the body joins it in sleeplessness and fever."

A Disbeliever

THE PROPHET said, "By God, he does not believe! By God, he does not believe!"

He was asked, "Of whom do you speak, O Messenger of God?"

The Prophet said, "One whose neighbor does not feel safe from his treachery."

A Neighbor's Gift

THE PROPHET used to say, "O believing women! Do not scorn a neighbor woman's gift, even if it is only sheep hooves."

The Behavior of Believers

THE PROPHET said, "Whoever believes in God and the Last Day should not wrong his neighbor. And whoever believes in God and the Last Day should treat his guest generously. And whoever believes in God and the Last Day should speak of good or keep silent."

All that Is Good and Fair

THE PROPHET said, "All that is objectively recognized as good and fair is sacred charity."

Character

THE PROPHET said, "The best of you are the most good-natured."

Intercede

WHENEVER A BEGGAR or a person in need came to the Prophet, he would say, "Intercede, and you will be rewarded; and God will bring about the divine will through the tongue of the Messenger of God."

Generosity

JĀBIR said, "The Prophet, may God bless him and grant him peace, never said no when asked for anything."

Courtesy

ANAS said, "The Prophet, may God bless him and grant him peace, was not one to speak abusively, to utter obscenities, or to curse."

Justice

THE PROPHET said, "When someone hurls the charge of iniquity or ingratitude at another, it comes right back to him if the other person is not like that."

Character Assassination

THE PROPHET said, "If anyone curses a believer, that is like murdering him; and if anyone accuses a believer of disbelief, that is like murdering him."

The Prophet also said, "A slanderer will not enter the Garden of Paradise."

Abstinence

THE PROPHET said, "God has no need of abstention from food and drink on the part of one who does not abstain from speaking falsely, acting thereupon, and stupid foolishness."

The Two-Faced

THE PROPHET said, "You will find among the worst people in God's perspective on the Day of Resurrection those who are two-faced, those who present one face to some and another face to others."

The Unforgiven

THE PROPHET said, "All of my people are pardoned but the blatantly shameless. An example of blatant shamelessness is when a man does something by night and then, come morning, in spite of the fact that God had screened him, he tells someone he did such-and-such a thing; whereas he had spent the night with God screening him, come daybreak he removes God's screen from himself!"

The End of Time

THE PROPHET said, "The Hour will not take place until two parties fight each other with one and the same aim."

Wages of Ingratitude

SOME PEOPLE from a certain tribe were adversely affected by the climate of Medina, so the Prophet allowed them to go to the camels given in charity and drink of their milk and [medicinal] urine. But when those people had recovered their health, they killed the herder and drove away the animals.

The Prophet sent a posse after them and had them brought back. Then he had their hands and feet cut off and their eyes seared, and left them in a stony area, biting on rocks.

A Time Is Coming

THE PROPHET said, "A time is coming to humankind when the individual does not care whether his gains are ethical or ill-gotten."

Angels at Arms

Sa'd ibn Abī Waqqāṣ related, "I saw the Prophet, may God bless him and grant him peace, on the day of the battle of Uhud; with him were two men fighting for him, dressed in white, who fought as fiercely as could be. I had never seen them before, nor did I see them after that."

The Protection of God

Once on an expedition the Prophet lay down for an afternoon nap in the shade of a tree, on which he hung his sword. When he awoke, he found a nomad standing over his head, holding his drawn sword.

The nomad challenged the Prophet, "Who will protect you from me?"

The Prophet answered, "God."

The nomad sheathed the sword and sat down. The Prophet did not punish him.

The Worst of Lies

The Prophet said, "Among the worst of lies are when someone claims to be the son of someone other than his father, when someone claims his eyes have seen what they have not seen, and when someone attributes to the Prophet of God something the Prophet has not said."

A Righteous Man

WHEN THE KING of Ethiopia died, the Prophet said to his people, "A righteous man has died today, so stand up and pray for your brother."

Marriage and Family

THE PROPHET asked Jābir, "Have you married?"

Jābir replied in the affirmative.

The Prophet asked, "Did you marry a virgin or an experienced woman?"

Jābir said, "An experienced woman."

The Prophet inquired, "Why not marry a young girl, who would play with you?"

Jābir said, "Messenger of God, my father was killed in the battle of Uhud, leaving nine daughters behind. So I have nine sisters, and I disliked adding another young girl untutored as they, preferring a woman who would groom them and take care of them."

The Original Sin

THE PROPHET said, "God Most High will say to the inmate of Hell whose punishment is lightest, 'If you had everything on earth, would you use it to redeem yourself?' The inmate will say, 'Yes!' And God will say, 'I asked you something easier than this while you were still in the loins of Adam: that you should not worship anything but God. Yet you insisted on worshiping other than God.' "

The Antichrist

THE PROPHET stood up among the people, praising God as God deserves praise, then mentioned the Antichrist and said, "I warn you all about him, for no prophet has failed to warn his people of him. Noah certainly warned his people, but I will tell you something about him that no prophet has ever told his people. Know that he is one-eyed; and God is not one-eyed."

The Prophet also said, "Shall I tell you a story about the Antichrist that no prophet has ever told his people? The fact is that the Antichrist is one-eyed, and he brings with him semblances of Paradise and Hell; but what he says is Paradise is in fact really Hell, so I warn you as Noah warned his people."

Sleep

THE PROPHET said, "Satan ties three knots at the back of the head of each one of you when you sleep, casting this suggestion on each knot in its place: 'The night is long for you, so sleep!' but if one awakens and remembers God, a knot is untied; and if one washes, another knot is untied. And if one prays, all the knots are untied. Then one gets up in the morning cheerful and lively, in good spirits. Otherwise, one gets up cranky and sluggish."

Soothsayers

THE PROPHET said, "The angels talk in the clouds about affairs that will come about on earth; the devils hear a word of it and put that in the ears of soothsayers, as you would put something in a bottle, and they add a hundred lies to it."

Producing Blessing

THE PROPHET said, "For whoever says, one hundred times a day, 'There is nothing to worship but God, the One, without partner: God's is the dominion, and all praise belongs to God; and God has power over everything,' there is the equivalent of freeing ten slaves, and a hundred good deeds are credited to him, and a hundred sins erased; and he has a sanctuary from the devil on that day until evening. And no one produces greater blessing than what he produces, except one who has done more than that."

Fairness

THE PROPHET said, "An ant stung one of the prophets, who then commanded that the ant nest be burned. But God inspired the prophet: 'If one ant bites you, you burn one of the communities that glorify God?' "

The Valor of the Prophet

On the day of the battle of Hunain, the Prophet dismounted from his mule when the pagans descended on him; he started saying, "I am the Prophet, no lie! I am the son of ʿAbdul Muṭṭalib." And no one was seen stronger or firmer on that day than the Prophet himself.

Injunctions to the Faithful

The Prophet said, "Emancipate the captive, feed the hungry, visit the sick."

The Bequest of the Prophet

The Prophet said, "My heirs will not divide up a single coin. Whatever I leave, besides support for my wives and provision for my workers, is charity."

Above and Below

When Saʿd thought himself more important than those below him in rank, the Prophet said to him, "Are you made triumphant and provided sustenance except by the powerless among you?"

Appearance and Reality

THE PROPHET said, "A person may be doing the deeds of the people of Paradise so far as society can see, while actually being one of the people of Hellfire. And a person may be doing the deeds of the people of Hellfire so far as society can see, while actually being one of the people of Paradise."

The Trench

THE PROPHET personally helped to dig the great trench at Medina. As he was carrying earth, he was heard to say, "If not for You, we would not have been guided, and we would not have given charity, and we would not have prayed. So cause tranquillity to descend upon us, and make our feet firm if we are not in the ascendant. For indeed people before have oppressed us, but whenever they wish to cause discord, we refuse."

Fasting

THE PROPHET said, "Whoever fasts a day in the way of God, God will keep his face from Hellfire for seventy autumns."

The Poverty of the Prophet

WHEN THE PROPHET died, he left nothing but his white mule, his armor, and a piece of land he dedicated to charity.

The Refuge of the Prophet

ON AN EXPEDITION, the Prophet was heard to say repeatedly, "O God, I take refuge with You from worry and grief, weakness and laziness, being bent by debt, and being overcome by men."

Profiteering

THE PROPHET related, "I dreamed that two men came to me and took me to a holy land, where we went on until we came to a river of blood, in which there stood a man. And by the riverside there was a man with stones in his hands, facing the man in the river. Now, when the man tried to come out of the river, the other man threw a stone into his mouth and made him go back to where he had been. And he proceeded to throw a stone into the man's mouth each and every time he tried to come out, making him return to the state he had been in.

"I then said, 'What is this?' "

The Prophet explained, "The one I saw in the river was a profiteer.' "

Fair Trade Practices

PEOPLE USED TO buy foodstuffs from the caravans in the lifetime of the Prophet, who sent someone to tell them not to sell it where they bought it, but to wait until they had transported it to the place where foodstuffs were sold.

The Prophet also forbade people to resell foodstuffs they had purchased unless and until they had received full measure and had paid the price in full.

Business Ethics

THE PROPHET said, "May God be merciful toward someone who is generous in buying, in selling, and in demanding payment."

Seven Destructive Things

THE PROPHET said, "Avoid the seven destructive things."
People asked, "What are they, O Messenger of God?"
The Prophet said, "Idolatry; sorcery; killing a person declared inviolable by God, except for a just reason; profiteering; consuming the property of an orphan; turning back when it is time to advance; and defaming chaste believing women who happen to be careless."

Consideration

ANAS related, "The Messenger of God, may God bless him and grant him peace, came to Medina without a single servant. So Abū Ṭalḥa took me to the Prophet and said, 'O Messenger of God, Anas is a smart boy, so let him serve you.'

"So I served the Prophet at home and abroad. Never did he ask me why I did anything I did, or why I did not do anything I did not do."

The Rewards of Paradise

THE PROPHET said, "No one who enters the Garden of Paradise would like to return to the world, not for anything on earth; except the martyr, who would return to the world and be killed ten times because of the Generosity he has seen."

The Way of God

THE PROPHET said, "No one whose feet get dusty in the way of God will be touched by Hellfire."

The Courage of the Prophet

ANAS said, "The Prophet, may God bless him and grant him peace, was the best of people, the bravest of people, and the most generous of people. Thus it was that when the people of Medina were alarmed, the Prophet rode ahead of them on a horse; and he said, 'We saw nothing to be alarmed at, but we sure found this horse to be a fast one.' "

Five Martyrs

THE PROPHET said, "There are five kinds of martyrs: one who dies of plague; one who dies of a disease of the stomach or intestines; one who drowns; one who is crushed in a collapsing building; and one who is martyred in the way of God."

Compassion

THE PROPHET went to a huge trench being dug in defense against attack, and saw the Emigrants* and the Helpers digging on a cold morning, since they had no slaves to do it for them. When he saw their exhaustion and hunger, the Prophet said, "O God, real life is the life of the Hereafter, so please forgive the Helpers and the Emigrants."

*The Emigrants are the early Meccan Muslims who emigrated to Medina (Yathrib) to escape persecution from the pagan Arabs.

The Whole Body

THE PROPHET said, "The example of one who observes the ordinances of God and one who disparages them is as that of people who draw lots for places on a ship, and some got the higher places while others got the lower places. Whenever those in the lower places wanted to get water to drink, they made their way past those who were above them. So they said, 'Let us make a hole in our part of the ship, so that we will not trouble those above us.' Now, if the others let them do what they wanted, it would destroy them all. But if they prevented them from doing so, they would save themselves, and would save everyone."

Ignoring Insidious Suggestion

THE PROPHET said, "God disregards for me whatever insidious suggestion occurs to my people, as long as they do not act on it or express it in speech."

Reception of Truth

THE PROPHET said, "The guidance and knowledge with which God has sent me are like abundant rain falling on the earth. Some of the earth is good soil that has absorbed the water and produces abundant grass and herbiage. Some of it is hard ground that holds back the water so that God may benefit people thereby, as they use it for drinking, watering animals, and irrigating tillage. And some of the rain falls on another portion of earth that is only a lowland, which neither holds water nor produces herbiage.

"The first simile is that of one who understands the religion of God, who is benefited by what God has sent me with, and who learns and teaches. The last simile is that of one who does not raise his head for it, and does not accept the guidance of God, with which I have been sent."

Every Night

THE PROPHET said, "Our Lord, Blessed and Exalted, descends every night to the earthly heaven when the last third of the night remains, saying, 'Who calls to Me, that I may answer? Who asks of Me, that I may give? Who seeks forgiveness of Me, that I may forgive?' "

Fasting

THE PROPHET said, "God Most High says, 'Fasting is for Me, and I reward it, for one leaves one's desire, food, and drink on My account; so fasting is a protective shield. And one who fasts has two joys: joy upon breaking the fast and joy on meeting God.' "

Grace and Mercy

ONCE WHEN THE PROPHET led a group of people in dawn prayer after a night rain, he faced them when the prayer was over and said, "Do you know what your Lord has said?"

They responded, "God and the Messenger know best!"

The Prophet said, "God has said, 'Some of My slaves have awakened as believers and disbelievers. Those who say Our rain was due to the grace and mercy of God are believers in Me and disbelievers in the stars. As for those who say it was due to such-and-such an atmospheric phenomenon, they are disbelievers in Me and believers in the stars.' "

Satisfaction

THE PROPHET said, "God will say to the people of Paradise, 'O people of Paradise!'

"And they will say, 'Here we are, O Lord, at Your service; felicity belongs to You, and all good is in Your hands!'

"Then God will say, 'Are you satisfied?'

"And they will say, 'Why should we not be satisfied, when You have bestowed on us what You have not bestowed on anyone in Your Creation?'

"Then God will say, 'Why don't I give you something even better than that?'

"They will say, 'O Lord! What is better than that?'

"And God will say, 'I will release you and never be angry with you anymore.' "

Night Vigil

WHEN THE PROPHET went to bed, he would say, "I die and live in Your name."

When he got up, he would say, "Thanks to God, Who has given us life after causing our death; and the Resurrection is to God."

When the Prophet arose at night for a vigil, he would say, "O God, all praise and thanks are Yours. You are the Light of the heavens and the earth, and all therein; and all praise and thanks belong to You. You are the caretaker of the heavens and the earth, and all therein; and all praise and thanks belong to You. You are the Truth, and Your promise is true, and Your word is true. The meeting with You is real, the Garden of Paradise is real, and Hellfire is real. The Hour is real, Prophethood is real, and Muḥammad is genuine. O God, I surrender to You, and I place my trust in You; I believe in You, and I turn to You in repentance. I argue for Your sake, and I appeal to You for judgment. So please forgive me for what I have brought to pass, and what I have left in my wake; what I have kept secret, and what I have disclosed. You are the one who sends forward, and You are the one who postpones. There is nothing worthy of worship but You."

Forgiveness

THE PROPHET said, "The best appeal for forgiveness is for one to say, 'O God, You are my Lord; there is no god but You. You created me, and I am Your slave; and I am faithful to my responsibility to You and my promise to You, as best I am able. I seek refuge with You from the ill of what I have done. I return to You with the blessings You have bestowed, and I return to You with the sins I have committed. So please forgive me, for no one forgives sin but You.' "

The Prophet added, "One who says this with certainty by day and then dies the same day before evening will be one of the people of Paradise. And one who says this with certainty by night and then dies before dawn will be one of the people of Paradise."

Bedtime Invocation

THE PROPHET said, "When you go to bed, wash as you do for prayer, then lie down on your right side and say, 'O God, I have surrendered my being to You. I entrust my affair to You, in hope and fear of You. There is no refuge or haven from You, except refuge with You and haven with You. I believe in Your word, which You have revealed, and in Your prophet, whom You have sent.' Then, if you die, you will die in the natural state of grace; so let this be the last thing you say."

Praise

ONCE A MAN was mentioned to the Prophet, and someone lavished fulsome praise on him. The Prophet said, "May God have mercy on you! You have cut the neck of your companion!"

The Prophet reiterated this several times, then said, "If any one of you must praise someone, then say, 'I think this and that,' if you really think so. For God is the one who takes account of the individual, and no one has better right to sanctify anyone than God."

Responsibility

THE PROPHET said, "Anyone whom God has placed in charge of a citizenry but who does not take care of them sincerely will not even get a scent of Paradise."

Deceiving the People

THE PROPHET said, "God forbids Paradise to any ruler of a Muslim citizenry who dies while he is deceiving them."

Authority

THE PROPHET also said, "We do not assign authority to one who asks for it, or to one who covets it."

Double Rewards

THE PROPHET said, "For any man who has a slave maiden whom he educates well, cultures and refines, then frees and marries, there is a double reward. And for any one of the people of the Book who believes his prophet and also believes me, there is a double reward. And for any slave who fulfills his duty to his master and also his duty to God, there is a double reward."

Sociability

THE PROPHET said, "Beware of suspicion, for suspicion is the falsest of talk. And do not snoop, and do not pry, and do not be divisive, but be brothers."

Magical Eloquence

'UMAR related that two men came from the East and lectured, whereat the Prophet said, "Some eloquence is magic indeed."

Portents

THE PROPHET said, "Among the portents of the Hour are the ending of knowledge and the prevalence of ignorance; the prevalence of adultery and the prevalence of drinking; and the decrease in men and increase in women to the point where there is but one supporter for fifty women."

The Questions of Caesar

THE PROPHET wrote to the Caesar of the Byzantine Empire, inviting him to Islam, sending a letter to him with Diḥya al-Kalbī. The Prophet directed him to present the letter to the governor of Busra, who would forward it to Caesar.

When God had relieved him of the Persian armies, Caesar walked from Emesa [in central Syria] to Jerusalem, out of gratitude to God for having inured him to trial. So when the letter of the Prophet reached him, Caesar read it and said, "Look for someone from his people around here, so that I may ask about this Messenger of God."

Now, it happened that Abū Sufyān was then in Syria with some men from the Quraish tribe who had come on business during the truce that then existed between the Prophet and the disbelievers of the Quraish.

Abū Sufyān later said, "The emissary of Caesar found us in a part of Syria, and he took me and my companions to Jerusalem. There we were brought to Caesar, who was sitting at his royal court, his crown on his head, around him the grandees of Byzantium."

Now, Caesar said to his interpreter, "Ask them who among them is closest in kinship to this man who claims to be a prophet."

Abū Sufyān [who was not a Muslim at the time] responded that he was nearest of them in kinship.

Caesar asked, "And what is the relationship between you and him?"

Abū Sufyān said, "He is a son of my paternal uncle."

Then Caesar said, "Bring him closer," and had Abū Sufyān's companions placed behind him, at his shoulders. Then he told his interpreter, "Tell his companions that I am going to question him about this man who claims to be a prophet; so if he tells a lie, immediately repudiate it as a lie."

Later Abū Sufyān admitted that he would have lied when asked about the Prophet, if not for the fact that he would have been shamed to have others spreading reports that he was a liar. So he told the truth.

Now, Caesar asked through his interpreter, "How is the lineage of this man among you?"

Abū Sufyān replied, "He is of noble descent among us."

Caesar asked, "And has any one of your people previously said what he has said?"

Abū Sufyān said, "No."

Caesar asked, "Had you found him a liar before he said what he has now said?"

Abū Sufyān said, "No."

Caesar asked, "Was any among his ancestors a king?"

Abū Sufyān replied, "No."

Caesar asked, "And do the highborn people listen to him, or the powerless among them?"

Abū Sufyān answered, "Rather the powerless."

Caesar asked, "And are they increasing or decreasing?"

Abū Sufyān replied, "Increasing."

Caesar asked, "And does anyone turn away discontent with his religion after having gone into it?"

Abū Sufyān said, "No."

Caesar asked, "Is he treacherous?"

Abū Sufyān replied, "No, but we are in a truce with him now, and we fear he may betray us." Later on, Abū Sufyān admitted that this was the closest he was able to come to putting in a bad word against Muḥammad.

Caesar went on, "Then have you fought each other?"

Abū Sufyān said, "Yes."

Caesar asked, "And how did your wars turn out?"

Abū Sufyān said, "Our contests have had alternating results; sometimes he wins over us, and other times we win over him."

Caesar asked, "What does he enjoin upon you?"

Abū Sufyān replied, "He enjoins us to worship God alone, not associating anything with the sole divinity. And he enjoins us not to worship the fetishes of our ancestors. He also enjoins us to pray, to give charity, and to be chaste; and to fulfill promises and discharge trusts."

When Abū Sufyān had said this, Caesar told his interpreter to say to him, "I asked you about his lineage among you, and you stated that he is of a sound lineage. And so were all prophets called forth from sound lineages of their people.

"Then I asked if anyone had said what he said before him, and you stated that none had. I would have said, if someone had said this before, that he was a man following something that had been said before him.

"And I asked you if you had found him a liar before he had said what he has said, and you stated that you had not. So I knew he would not lie about God if he did not lie about humans.

"And I asked you if any of his ancestors was a king, and you stated that none had been. I would have said, if any of his ancestors had been a king, that he was seeking the kingdom of his ancestors.

"And I asked you if the highborn people followed him, or the powerless ones; and you stated that it is the powerless. And they are the followers of the Messengers.

"And I asked you if they were increasing or decreasing, and you stated that they were increasing. And so it is with Faith, until it is complete.

"And I asked you if anyone turns away disaffected with his religion after having gone into it, and you stated that none did; and so it is with Faith, with which no one is displeased when its cheerfulness mixes into hearts.

"And I asked you if he acts treacherously, and you stated that he does not. And so it is with all Messengers; they do not act treacherously.

"And I asked you if you fight with each other, and you stated that you did, and that your fortunes in war alternated, now in his favor, now in yours. And so are all Messengers tried, and final victory will be his.

"And I asked you what he enjoins upon you, and you

stated that he enjoins you to worship God, and not to associate anything with God, and not to worship the fetishes of your ancestors. And he enjoins you to pray, to give charity, to be chaste, to keep promises, and to fulfill trusts. And this is the description of a prophet.

"I knew he would appear, but I did not know he would be from among you. If what you have said is true, he will soon rule the ground beneath these two feet of mine. If I could expect to reach him, I would take it upon myself to go and meet him; and if I were with him, I would wash his feet."

Then Caesar called for the letter of the Prophet, and it was read aloud. In it was this:

> In the name of God, the Compassionate, the Merciful. From Muḥammad, slave and messenger of God, to Heraclius, ruler of Byzantium. Peace upon all who follow Guidance.
>
> Now then, I call you with the call to submission to God. Surrender to God, and you will be safe. Surrender to God, and God will give you a double reward. If you turn away, then the misdeeds of the peasants will be your fault.
>
> And, people of the Book, come to a Word common to both of us, that we worship only God and do not associate anything with God, and that none of us takes any for lords but God. And if they turn away, then say, "Witness that we have surrendered to God."

Now, when Heraclius Caesar finished his speech, a cry arose from the grandees of Byzantium around him. So great was their uproar that Abū Sufyān did not understand what they said; but he and his companions were ejected.

When the men of the Quraish had left the court of the Byzantine emperor and were alone, Abū Sufyān said to them, "The affair of Muḥammad has grown powerful; even the king of the pale people fears him!"

Later, Abū Sufyān related, "I lay low, by God, certain that the affair of Muḥammad would emerge triumphant, until God brought my heart into Islam in spite of my aversion to it."

The Death of a Prophet

WHEN THE PROPHET was still in good health, he used to say, "No prophet dies until he is shown his place in the Garden of Paradise; then he is enlivened or allowed to make a choice."

When the Prophet was suffering and his demise approached, he swooned with his head resting on 'Ā'isha's thigh. When he came to his senses, he looked upward and said, "O God, with the highest companion!"

Then he died.

Seeing God

MASRŪQ asked 'Ā'isha, "Did the blessed Muḥammad see God?"

'Ā'isha said, "I am horrified by what you say! If anyone

tells you one of three things, he has lied. Anyone who tells you Muḥammad saw God has lied."

And ʿĀʾisha recited: "No vision can comprehend God, but God comprehends all vision. And God is most subtle, perfectly aware" [6:103].

"And it is not for a human being to be spoken to by God, except by inspiration, or from behind a veil" [42:51].

ʿĀʾisha continued, "And anyone who tells you that Muḥammad knows what is to be on the morrow has lied."

Then ʿĀʾisha recited: "No soul knows what it will earn on the morrow" [31:34].

ʿĀʾisha went on, "And anyone who tells you Muḥammad concealed or withheld anything has lied."

Then ʿĀʾisha recited: "O Messenger, deliver the message that has been sent down to you from God" [5:70].

Finally she added, "But he did see the blessed Gabriel in his own form twice."

Love of God

THE MESSENGER OF GOD said, "God the Exalted has said, 'I declare war on anyone who antagonizes a friend of Mine. And when a servant of Mine approaches Me through what is most beloved to me of what I have enjoined on him, and My servant does not cease to approach Me through extra efforts until I love him, then when I love him I am the ear by which he hears, and the eye by which he sees, and the hand by which he grasps, and the foot by which he walks. And if he asks of Me, I give to him. And if he seeks refuge with Me, I certainly give him protection.' "

Nearness to God

THE PROPHET related that his Lord, Great and Glorious, said, "When the devotee becomes a foot closer to Me, I become a yard closer to him. And when he gets a yard closer to Me, I get a fathom closer to him. And when he walks to Me, I run to him."

Striving

ʿĀʾISHA RELATED, "When it came to the last ten days of Ramadan, the Messenger of God used to stay awake all night, urging his family to wakefulness too, while striving energetically."

Strength and Weakness

THE MESSENGER OF GOD said, "The strong believer is better and more beloved of God than the weak believer, though there is good in each. Strive for what benefits you, and ask God for help, and don't weaken. And if something happens to you, don't say, 'If only I had done this or that it would have turned out thus and so.' Instead, say, 'God has so determined, and God does what God will.' For 'if only' introduces the work of Satan, insidious suggestion."

What Remains

THE MESSENGER OF GOD said, "Three things follow the deceased: his family, his wealth, and his works. Thus two return while one remains. His family and his wealth return, while his works remain."

Heaven and Hell

THE PROPHET said, "The garden of Paradise is closer to you than your shoelace; and so is the fire of Hell."

Prostration

THAUBAN, a companion of the Messenger of God, said, "I heard the Messenger of God say, 'You ought to perform prostrations a lot; for every time you prostrate yourself before God, God elevates you a step thereby, and decreases a fault in you thereby.' "

God and Humanity

THE PROPHET related that God, Exalted and Blessed, said, "O My servants, I have forbidden Myself injustice, and have made it forbidden to you; so do not be unjust.

"O My servants, all of you are lost but those I guide; so seek guidance of Me, and I will guide you.

"O My servants, all of you are hungry but those I feed; so seek sustenance from Me, and I will feed you.

"O My servants, all of you are naked but those I clothe; so seek clothing from Me, and I will clothe you.

"O My servants, you make mistakes night and day, yet I forgive all misdeeds; so seek forgiveness from me, and I will pardon you.

"O My servants, you cannot do Me any harm, and you cannot provide Me any benefit.

"O My servants, even if the first of you and the last of you and the humans among you and the spirits among you were like the man with the most conscientious heart among you, that would not add anything to My dominion.

"O My servants, even if the first of you and the last of you and the humans among you and the spirits among you were like the man with the most dissolute heart of anyone among you, that would not take anything way from My dominion.

"O My servants, even if the first of you and the last of you and the humans among you and the spirits among you stood on one plateau and asked of Me, and I granted every human being what he asked, that would not diminish what I have, except as much as might a needle dipped in the sea.

"O My servants, it is only your deeds that I charge to your account; and then I set them out before you in full. So whoever meets with good should praise God, and whoever finds anything else should blame none but himself."

Forgiveness

THE PROPHET said, "God keeps forgiving a person until one reaches the age of sixty."

Daily Practices

THE MESSENGER OF GOD said, "Cleanliness is part of faith.

"Praising God fills the balance; glorifying and praising God fills what is between the heavens and the earth, and prayer is light.

"Charity is an evidence, and patience is a radiance.

"The Qur'ān is an argument for you or against you.

"Everyone starts the day selling his soul, and either frees it or ruins it."

The State of the Believer

THE MESSENGER OF GOD said, "The state of the believer is wonderful; everything in it is good for him, and for no one else but the believer. If happiness comes his way, he is grateful and so it is good for him; and if adversity strikes him, he is patient and so it is good for him."

Tyranny and Faith

THE MESSENGER OF GOD related, "There was a king of yore who had a magician. When he grew old, the magician said to the king, 'I have gotten old; send me a youth that I may teach him magic.' So the king sent him a youth to instruct.

"Now on his way there was a monk, and the youth sat down with him and listened to him talk. He thought the monk's talk was wonderful, and so every time he passed by the monk on his way to the magician he would sit with him. Then when he'd go to the magician, the magician would beat him.

"The youth complained to the monk about this. The monk said, 'When you are afraid of the magician, say your family detained you; and when you are afraid of your family, say the magician detained you.'

"The youth was following this course of action when by and by he came upon an enormous beast that was blocking people's way. The youth said, 'Today I'll know who is superior, the magician or the monk.' Then he took up a stone and said, 'O my God, if the business of the monk is dearer to You than that of the magician, then slay this beast so that the people may pass.' Then he hurled the stone and killed the beast; and the people went their way.

"Now the youth went to the monk and informed him of this. The monk said to him, 'My son, today you are better than I; you have attained in actual fact what I only see. But you will surely be tested. If you are tried, don't give me away.'

"Then the youth was healing the blind and the leprous, and treating people for the general run of diseases.

"Now one of the king's courtiers, who had become blind, heard of this youth. He went to him with many gifts and said, 'All this is yours if you heal me.'

"The youth said, 'I do not heal anyone; it is God alone, the Exalted, who heals. So if you believe in God the Exalted, I will pray to God, and God will heal you.'

"So the courtier put his faith in God, and God healed him.

"Then the courtier went to the king and sat with him as he used to do. The king said to him, 'Who restored your sight to you?'

"The courtier said, 'My Lord.'

"The king said, 'So you have a lord besides me?'

"The courtier said, 'My Lord, and your Lord, is God.'

"Then the king had him arrested and tortured until he informed on the youth.

"Now the king had the youth arrested and tortured until he informed on the monk.

"Now the monk was arrested and told to renounce his religion. This he refused. So a saw was called for and placed on the center of the monk's head, cutting it asunder.

"Then the king's courtier was summoned and told to renounce his religion. He refused, and his head was also sawed in half.

"Then the youth was summoned and told to renounce his religion. He refused, so the king turned him over to a band of his men and said, 'Take him to such and such a mountain, and go up the mountain with him. When you reach the top, throw him off unless he has renounced his religion.'

"So they took him up the mountain, whereat he said, 'My God, save me from them by whatever means You will.' Then the mountain convulsed with them, and they slipped and fell.

"The youth walked back to the king, who said to him, 'What happened to the men with you?'

"The youth said, 'God the Exalted saved me from them.'

"Then the king turned him over to another band of his men, telling them, 'Take him out to the middle of the sea, and dump him overboard if he doesn't renounce his religion.'

"So they took him, but he said, 'My God, save me from them, by any means You will.' Then the boat capsized and they drowned.

"The youth walked back to the king, who said, to him, 'What happened to the men with you?'

"The youth said, 'God the Exalted saved me from them.' Then he told the king, 'You will not be able to kill me until you do what I tell you to.'

"The king said, 'What is that?'

"The youth said, 'Gather all the people on a common ground, and set me on a tree stump. Then take an arrow from my quiver, place it in the center of the bow, then say, 'In the name of God, Lord of all worlds,' and shoot me. When you have done that, then you will kill me.'

"So the king gathered all the people on a plain, set the youth on a stump, took an arrow from his quiver, set it in the middle of the bow, said, 'In the name of God, Lord of all worlds,' and shot. The arrow hit the youth in the temple; he put his hand to his temple and died.

"Now the people declared, 'We believe in the youth's God.'

"The king was approached and told, 'Do you see—what you feared has, by God, actually happened to you—the people believe in God.'

"So the king ordered trenches dug along the streets and fires kindled in them. Then he declared, 'Whoever does not renounce his religion I will have pushed into the fire, or will be told to jump in.'

"And that's what they did, until there came up a woman who had a boy with her. When she hesitated to get into the fire, the boy said to her, 'Bear up, mother, for you are in the right.' "

Resignation and Paradise

THE PROPHET said, "God the Exalted says, 'For a believing servant of Mine who accepts it when I take one of his dear ones from among the people of the world, I have no reward but the garden of Paradise.' "

Submission, Affliction, and Pardon

THE PROPHET said, "No affliction afflicts one who submits to the will of God—no illness, no anxiety, no sorrow, no injury, no distress, nor any complaint one may complain of—but God pardons some of his faults for it."

Hurry and Complaint

ABŪ ʿABDULLĀH KHABBAB BIN AL-ARAT said, "We complained to the Messenger of God as he was reclining on his cloak in the shade of the Kaʿba, 'Won't you ask for help for us? Won't you pray for us?' "

He said, "There were those before you who were not discouraged from their religion when they were seized and buried in pits and had their heads sawed in half or combed with an iron comb until their flesh was removed from their bones. God will complete this affair, by God, to the point where a rider can travel from the plains to the seashore without fear of anything but God and wolves after his sheep. But you are in a hurry."

Affliction and Good

THE MESSENGER OF GOD said, "When God wants good for a mortal, God hastens affliction in this world; and when God wants ill for a mortal, God leaves him be with his sin until his soul is taken on the day of resurrection."

Power

THE MESSENGER OF GOD said, "The powerful one is not the one who overthrows others, but the one who controls himself in anger."

Anger

THE PROPHET said, "Whoever suppresses and conceals anger when he is able to express and act on it will be called by God above all creatures on the day of resurrection, and given his choice of the virgins of Paradise, just as he desires."

Testing

THE MESSENGER OF GOD said, "The testing of a believer, male or female, in respect to one's person, children, and property will not cease until one meets God the Exalted unburdened by any sin."

Duty and Right

THE MESSENGER OF GOD said, "After me there will surely be selfishness and affairs you will disdain."

People said, "Then what do you tell us to do?"

He said, "Execute the duty that is incumbent upon you, and ask God for the right that is due to you."

Truthfulness

THE PROPHET said, "Truthfulness leads to probity, and probity leads to Paradise. And a man will persist in truthfulness until he is confirmed truthful in the sight of God.

"Falsehood leads to immorality, and immorality leads to the Inferno. And a man persists in falsehood until he is confirmed deceitful in the sight of God."

Doubt and Disquiet

THE MESSENGER OF GOD said, "Leave aside whatever causes you doubts or misgivings, in favor of what does not cause you doubts or misgivings. For truth is peace of mind, while falsehood is mental disquiet."

Spoils of War

THE MESSENGER OF GOD said, "One of the prophets— may the prayer and peace of God be upon him—went on a military expedition. He announced to his people, 'Let no man follow me who has gotten married but not yet consummated the marriage, and no one who is building houses but has not yet raised their roofs, and no one who has purchased livestock in anticipation of their offspring.' "

Then he went on the expedition, drawing near to the city at the time of the daybreak prayer, or earlier, whereupon he said to the sun, "You are directed, certainly, but I was directed too," and he prayed, "Our God, detain her on our account." Then the sun was delayed until God had granted him victory.

Then the spoils were collected and fire set to them to burn them; but it didn't consume them. So the prophet said, "There is pilfering of spoils going on among you. Let a man from each tribe pledge allegiance to me." As they did so, the hand of one man stuck to the hand of the prophet. He said, "The pilfering is going on among your people, so let your tribe pledge allegiance to me." Then the hands of two or three men stuck to the hand of the prophet; he said, "The pilfering is going on among you." Then they brought a head resembling the head of a cow, made of gold; he put it in the fire with the spoils, and the fire consumed them.

"So spoils of war were not lawful for anyone before us. Then God made spoils of war lawful to us on seeing our weakness and disability."

Mindfulness

THE PROPHET said, "Be mindful of God, and you will find God in front of you. Acknowledge God in ease, and God will acknowledge you in distress. And know that what misleads you will never enable you to do right, and what enables you to do right will never mislead you. And know that help comes with patience, and that relief comes with distress; and that with difficulty comes ease."

Acknowledgment

THE PROPHET told a story, "There were three Israelites, a leper, a bald man, and a blind one. In order to test them, God sent an angel to them."

The angel came to the leper and said, "What would you like most?"

He said, "A good complexion and good skin, and riddance of that for which people have considered me unclean."

Then the angel passed his hand over him, and his uncleanness disappeared from him, and he acquired a good complexion.

Now the angel said, "And what would you like most to have?"

He said, "Camels."

So he was given a she-camel in her tenth month of pregnancy. He said, "God bless you for this."

Then the angel came to the bald man and said, "What would you like most?"

He said, "Nice hair, and riddance of this condition for which people dislike me."

Then the angel passed his hand over him, and his baldness disappeared as he acquired a full head of hair.

Now the angel said to him, "And what would you like to have?"

He said, "Cattle."

So he was given a pregnant cow. And he said, "God bless you for this."

Then the angel came to the blind man and said, "What would you like most?"

He said, "That God may restore my vision so I might see people."

So the angel passed his hand over him and God restored his eyesight.

Now the angel said, "And what would you like to have?"

He said, "Sheep."

So he was given a pregnant ewe.

The former two animals gave birth, and so did this latter one; eventually one of the men had a valley full of camels, one had a valley full of cattle, and one had a valley full of sheep.

Then the angel came to the leper in disguise and said, "I am a poor man, at the end of my rope on my journey, without recourse this day except to God and to you. I ask you—by the One who gave you a good complexion, good skin, and wealth—for a camel whereby I may make it to the end of my journey."

But the man said, "I have many obligations."

Then the angel said, "I seem to know you. Weren't you a leper, shunned by society as unclean, impoverished? And did not God give to you?"

He said, "I simply inherited this wealth, grown generation after generation."

The angel said, "You are a liar. May God make you as you were."

Then the angel came to the formerly bald man in disguise and spoke to him as he had the former leper. And the formerly bald man replied as had the former leper. So the angel said, "You are a liar. May God make you as you were."

Then the angel also came to the formerly blind man and said, "I am a poor man, on the road, at the end of my rope on my journey, with no resort this day but to God and to you. I ask you—by the One who restored your vision—for a sheep to tide me over on my way."

The man said, "I used to be blind, but God restored my eyesight. Take whatever you want, and leave what you will. For by God I will give you no trouble about anything you take today for the sake of God."

The angel said, "Keep what you have; for you were only being tested. God is pleased with you, and displeased with the other two."

Intelligence and Incompetence

THE PROPHET said, "The intelligent one is the one who holds himself responsible and works for what is after death. And the incompetent one is the one who indulges himself in pursuit of personal desire and importunes God."

Minding Your Own Business

THE MESSENGER OF GOD said, "Part of the excellence of one's Islam is avoiding involvement in what does not concern one."

The Noble Ones

ABŪ HURAIRAH relates, "The Messenger of God was asked, 'Who are the most noble of the people?' "

He said, "The most conscientious of them."

They said, "This is not what we are asking you about."

He said, "Then it would be Joseph, prophet of God, a son of a prophet of God who was a son of a prophet of God who was a son of Abraham, the Friend of God."

They said, "This is not what we are asking you about."

He said, "Then are you asking me about the original nobility of the Arabs? The best of them in ignorance are the best of them in Islam when they have come to understanding."

A Supplication

THE PROPHET used to say, "O God, I ask you for guidance, conscience, decency, and self-sufficiency."

The Guiltless

THE MESSENGER OF GOD said, "All peoples appeared to me, and I saw prophets accompanied by a group, and prophets accompanied by one or two people, and prophets who had no one with them at all. Then an enormous multitude stood out to me, and I thought they were my community; but I was told, 'This is Moses and his people; but look to the horizon,' and when I looked there was another enormous multitude. Then I was told, 'Look to the other horizon,' and there too was an enormous multitude. Now I was told, '*This* is your community; and among them are seventy thousand who will enter Paradise without any account or any chastisement.' "

Then the Prophet got up and went into his house. Now the people became engrossed in the question of who would be the ones to enter Paradise without reckoning or castigation. Some supposed they would be those who associated with the Messenger of God. Some said they may be those who were born into Islam and had never been polytheists.

And as they spoke of things, the Messenger of God came out to them and asked what they had been discussing. When they told him, he said, "They are those who do not use magic or incantations, or have others employ them on their behalf, and do not consult omens, but trust in God, their Sustainer."

A Prayer of the Prophet

THE MESSENGER OF GOD used to say, "O my God, I resign myself to You, and I believe in You. I trust in You, and to You I turn; and by You I prevail. O my God, I take refuge in Your might—there is no deity but You—lest You allow me to get lost. You are the Living, who never dies, while spirits and humans do die."

Count on God

IBN ʿABBĀS said, "We count on God, who is perfectly reliable—this is what Abraham said when he was thrown into fire, and this is also what Muḥammad said when they told him the people had ganged up against him and he should fear them. That increased the faith of the Muslims, who said, 'We count on God, who is perfectly reliable.'"

Hearts like Birds

THE PROPHET said, "People whose hearts are like the hearts of birds will enter the garden of Paradise."

Under the Sword

JĀBIR related, "We went on an expedition with the Prophet, toward Nejd; and came back together with him when the Messenger of God returned. Now midday came

upon them in a valley full of thorny shrubs; the Messenger
of God halted there, and the people separated to look for
shade in the bush. The Messenger of God camped under a
gum-acadia, where he hung up his sword.

"We also took a nap. Suddenly we heard the Messenger
of God calling us. We found a desert Arab with him. He
said, 'This man turned my sword on me while I was sleeping; when I awoke he had it in his hand, drawn.' He said,
'Who will protect you from me?' I said, 'God three
times.'"

The Prophet did not have him punished.

According to another version, Jābir said, "We were out
with the Messenger of God when we came upon a shady
tree. We left it for the Messenger of God. One of the polytheists came, and the sword of the Messenger of God was
hanging on the tree; he drew it and said, 'Do you fear me?'
The Messenger of God said, 'No.' The idolater said, 'But
who will protect you from me?' The Messenger of God
said, 'God.'"

According to Abū Bakr al Ismaili's account, "When the
desert Arab said, 'Who will protect you from me?' The
Prophet said, 'God,' and the sword fell from the man's
hand. The Messenger of God picked up the sword and said,
'Who will protect *you* from *me*?'" The man said, 'Be a good
captor.'

The Prophet then said, "Do you testify that there is no
deity but God, and that I am the messenger of God?"

He said, "No, but I promise you I won't fight you, or side with people who fight you."

So the Prophet let him go on his way.

When the desert Arab reached his comrades he said, "I have come to you from the best of men."

Trust in God

THE MESSENGER OF GOD said, "If you really trusted in God as God should be trusted, God would sustain you as God sustains the birds—they go out in the morning hungry, and come back to rest in the evening full."

Bedtime Prayer

BARA'A BIN 'AZIB related that the Messenger of God said to him, "When you go to bed, say, 'O my God, I submit my soul to You, and I turn my face to You, and I entrust my affairs to You, and I commit my burden to You, longing for You yet dreading You: there is no shelter from You, nor haven, except with You. I believe in Your Book, which You have revealed, and Your prophets, whom you have sent.

"Then if you die that night, you will die in innocence; and if you wake up the next morning, you will encounter good."

Prayers on Leaving the House

ACCORDING TO UMM SALAMA, Mother of the Believers, wife of the Prophet, "When the Prophet left the house, he used to say, 'In the name of God; I trust in God. O my God, I take refuge with You from losing the way or being misled; or slipping into error or being tripped up; or doing injustice or being abused; or acting foolishly or being treated foolishly.' "

The Messenger of God said, "Whoever says, on leaving his house, 'In the name of God; I trust in God. There is no power and no capability except through God,' he will be answered, 'You are guided; and you are sufficed; and you are protected,' and Satan will retreat from him."

A Statement of Islam

SUFYĀN BIN 'ABDULLĀH related, "I said to the Messenger of God, 'Tell me a statement on Islam such that I need ask no one else but you about it.' He told me, 'Say, "I believe in God," and be upright.' "

Salvation by Acts

THE MESSENGER OF GOD said, "Focus closely, and realize that none of you will be saved by his acts."

Some said, "Not even you, Messenger of God?"

He said, "Not even me, unless God conceals my flaws with divine mercy and grace."

Work without Delay

THE MESSENGER OF GOD said, "Embark upon works without delay, being as how there are trials like portions of the dark night, when a man is a believer in the morning but a scoffer by bedtime, or is a believer one evening but a scoffer the next day. He sells his faith for the sake of something that happens to him."

Charity in Time

A MAN came to the Prophet and said, "O Messenger of God, what charity has the greatest reward?"

He said, "When you give alms when you are in good health and reluctant to give, fearing poverty and hoping for wealth.

"And do not wait until the last gasp when you say 'so-and-so gets this, so-and-so gets that,' for it already belongs to that so-and-so."

Don't Wait

THE MESSENGER OF GOD said, "Undertake good works before seven things happen: distracting poverty, corrupting wealth, debilitating illness, befuddling senility, final death, the Antichrist—and evil is the invisible one who waits and watches—or the final hour, which is more calamitous and more painful."

Certainty

THE PROPHET said, "Call on me in regard to anything I have not mentioned to you. People before you were only destroyed by their excessive questioning and their differences regarding their prophets. So when I forbid you something, then avoid it; and when I enjoin something on you, then carry it out to the extent of your ability."

An Admonition

THE PROPHET stood up and addressed the people, "O people, you are to be gathered to God Most High barefoot, naked, and uncircumcised: 'As We began the first creation, so shall We repeat it; it is a promise binding on Us, and We will indeed do it.' [*The Prophets 104*]

"Note that the first of creatures to be clothed on the day of resurrection will be Abraham. And note that some people of my community will be brought and taken to the left, and I will say, 'O my Lord, these are my companions.'

"And it will be said, 'You are unaware of what they started after you.'

"Then I will say as did the pious devotee, 'I was watching over them as long as I was among them; then when You took my life, you were the one watching over them. And You are witness to everything. If You punish them, that is because they are Your servants; and if You forgive them, that is because You are the epitome of power and wisdom.'

"And I will be told, 'They never stopped turning on their heels since you departed from them.' "

Revelation and Reception

Abū Huraira related, "When this was revealed to the Messenger of God: 'To God belongs whatever is in the heavens and whatever is on earth; and whether you reveal what is in your souls or conceal it, God calls you to account for it,' [*The Cow 284*], that was unbearable to the companions of the Messenger of God."

So they came to the Prophet, knelt down on their knees, and said, "O Messenger of God, there are works we can do—prayer, struggle, fasting, charity—but now this sign has been revealed to you, which is beyond our capacity."

The Messenger of God said, "Do you want to speak as spoke the people of the Two Testaments before you—'We hear and we resist'? Say, rather, 'We hear and we obey; may you pardon us, our Sustainer, for it is to You that we return.' "

Then when the people had recited that, and their tongues had become accustomed to it, God Most High revealed right after it, "The messenger believes in what was revealed to him from his Sustainer; and the believers each believe in God, and God's angels, and God's testaments, and God's messengers—we do not make a distinction among any of God's messengers." They said, "We hear and we obey. May You pardon us, our Sustainer, for it is to You we return."

Then when they had practiced that, God Most High abrogated it, revealing, "God does not impose anything on a being but what it can bear—one gets what one deserves and is responsible for what one has done. Our Sustainer, do not blame us if we forget or make a mistake."

"Yes."

"Our Sustainer, do not impose on us a burden like that You imposed on those before us."

"Yes."

'Our Sustainer, do not burden us with what we cannot bear.'

"Yes."

"And pardon us, and forgive us, and have mercy on us: You are our protector, so help us against people who disbelieve."

"Yes."

Custom and Credit

Aʙū Aᴍʀᴜ relates, "We were with the Messenger of God in the forenoon when a group of people came who were naked, with strips of rent woolen cloaks wrapped clumsily around their heads, wearing their swords around their necks. They were from the Mudar tribe."

The face of the Messenger of God fell on seeing the poverty of these people. He went inside, then came out and had Bilāl give the call to prayer. After praying, he gave a speech citing, "O people, be conscious of your Sustainer, who created you from one soul," and so on, until the end of the verse, "for God is watching over you." And another verse which is on the aftermath of the day of resurrection, "O you who believe, be conscious of God, and let each individual soul pay attention to what it brings forth for the morrow." The Prophet concluded, "Let each man give charity from his cash, his clothing, his wheat, his dates, even be it half a date."

Then one of the Helpers came with a bundle so heavy he could hardly carry it. Then people followed in succession until I saw two heaps of food and clothing. And I saw the face of the Messenger of God beaming, shining like gold. Then the Messenger of God said, "Whoever introduces a good custom in Islam will have its reward, as well as the reward of those who act on it after him, without that diminishing their rewards at all. And whoever introduces a bad custom in Islam is responsible for its burdens, as well as the burden of those who act on it after him, without that reducing their burden of responsibility at all."

Influencing Others

THE MESSENGER OF GOD said, "Whoever calls to guidance has a reward equal to the rewards of those who follow him, without that diminishing their rewards in any way. And whoever calls to error bears a burden of guilt equal to the sins of those who follow him, without that diminishing their guilt in any way.

Guidance and Action

THE MESSENGER OF GOD said, "One who shows the way to good has a reward equal to that of the one who carries it out."

Religion and Goodwill

THE PROPHET said, "Religion is goodwill."

He was asked, "Toward whom?"

He said, "Toward God, and toward the Book of God, and toward the Messenger of God, and toward the imams of the Muslims, and toward their communities."

The Least Requirement

THE MESSENGER OF GOD said, "If any of you sees something reprehensible, let him amend it by his hand. And if that is not possible, then by his speech. And if that is not possible, then by his heart. And that is the least that faith requires."

Decline in Faith

THE PROPHET said, "Every prophet sent by God to a people before me had disciples and companions among his people who followed his example and were guided by his direction. Then others came after them who said what they didn't do and did what they were not told. Whoever fights them with his hand is a believer, and whoever fights them by his heart is a believer. And after that there is not a mustard-seed of faith left."

Rulers

THE PROPHET said, "Rulers will be constituted over you whom you will both recognize and despise. One who disapproves is innocent, and one who ignores is safe; but not one who gladly follows along."

People said, "Shall we fight them, Messenger of God?"

He said, "Not as long as they keep up prayer among you."

Struggle

THE PROPHET was asked, "What is the most blessed struggle?"

He said, "Speaking truth to an oppressive ruler."

Preaching and Practice

THE MESSENGER OF GOD said, "A certain man will be brought forth on the day of resurrection and thrown into Hellfire, whereupon his guts will spill out, and he will go round and round with them like a donkey round a mill."

Then the people in Hell will gather around him and say, "Hey, what happened to you? Didn't you use to enjoin right and forbid wrong?"

And he will say, "Yes, but I used to enjoin right without doing it myself, and I used to forbid wrong even while doing it myself."

Crossing Over

THE MESSENGER OF GOD said, "God, Blessed and Exalted, will gather humanity together, and the faithful will be standing near Paradise. They will go to Adam and say, 'O Father, seek to have Paradise opened to us.' He will say, 'Was it anything but the crime of your father that got you ejected from Paradise? I am not the one for that. Go to my son Abraham, Friend of God.'

"So they will go to Abraham, but he will say, 'I am not the one for that. I am only a friend from way back. Apply to Moses, to whom God spoke directly.' So then they will go to Moses, but he will say, 'I am not the one for that. Go to Jesus, word and spirit of God.' But Jesus will say, 'I am not the one for that.'

"So then they will go to Muḥammad, who will stand up and be given permission for this. Then fidelity and kinship will stand by both sides of the road, right and left, and the first of you will cross over like lightning."

Abū Huraira asked what the lightning crossing will be like. The Prophet said, "Haven't you seen how lightning flashes and recurs in the blink of an eye? Next will be like the flight of birds, then the charge of men, their deeds carrying them along. And your prophet will be standing at the wayside, saying, 'My Lord, grant safety, grant safety.' Eventually the practices of the devotees will weaken, until someone comes who can only crawl. And on both sides of the way are hooks, on which are suspended those designated for punishment. One who is only grazed is saved, while one who gets jammed is in Hell."

Beware

THE MESSENGER OF GOD said, "Beware of injustice, for injustice will become a multitude of shadows on the day of resurrection. And beware of avarice, for avarice destroyed those who were before you, carrying them away to the point where they shed their blood and thought their taboos permissible to them."

Misappropriation of Land

THE MESSENGER OF GOD said, "One who misappropriates land, or falsifies the registration, even be it so much as a span, will have seven earths hung 'round his neck."

The Punishment of God

THE MESSENGER OF GOD said, "God gives the wrongdoer plenty of time, but then when God seizes him, God does not let him get away."

Then he recited, "And such is the punishment of your Lord, when punishing unjust peoples; indeed the punishment of God is painful, severe." [11.102]

Taking Without Right

THE PROPHET put a certain man in charge of charity. When the man arrived, he said, "This is for all of you, and this is given to me."

Then the Messenger of God stood up in the pulpit, praised and extolled God, then said, "Now then, I put a man from among you in charge of a task God has entrusted to me; then he comes back and says, 'This is for all of you, and this is a gift that has been given me.' If he was right, why didn't he stay in his parents' house and wait for his gift to come to him? By God, whatever any one of you takes without a right, he will meet God the Exalted on the day of resurrection carrying it."

Injustice by Oath

THE MESSENGER OF GOD said, "Whoever takes the right of a Muslim by his oath has already been sentenced by God to Hellfire and forbidden the garden of Paradise."

Someone asked, "Even if it is an insignificant thing?"

The Messenger replied, "Even if it is a toothpick."

Embezzlement

THE MESSENGER OF GOD said, "If we put one of you at the head of an operation and he conceals as much as a needle or more from us, that is embezzlement, for which he will pay on the day of resurrection."

Bankruptcy

THE MESSENGER OF GOD said, "Do you know who is bankrupt?"

People said, "Among us, a bankrupt is one who has no money and no property."

The Messenger of God said, "A bankrupt among my people is one who goes to the day of resurrection with prayer, fasting, and charity, but goes having abused someone, and having defamed someone, and having consumed someone's property, and having shed someone's blood, and having beaten someone. So each one is given something from his merits, and if his merits run out before his debt is judged, the others' sins will be taken from them and cast on him; and then he will be flung into Hellfire."

The Scope of the Religion

THE MESSENGER OF GOD said, "A believer is still within the scope of his religion as long as he does not shed forbidden blood."

Mismanagement

THE MESSENGER OF GOD said, "There are men who mishandle God's property; for them is Hellfire on the day of resurrection."

The Body of Believers

THE MESSENGER OF GOD said, "The believers, in their mutual friendship, compassion, and attachment, are like the body; when one of its members suffers, the whole body is adversely affected for its sake, with sleeplessness and fever."

Compassion

THE MESSENGER OF GOD said, "Whoever has no compassion for people, God has no compassion for him."

Consideration

THE MESSENGER OF GOD said, "I stand for prayer wanting to prolong it, but then I hear the cry of a child, so I abridge the prayer, disliking to inconvenience its mother."

Brotherhood

THE MESSENGER OF GOD said, "A Muslim is the brother of a Muslim; he does not wrong him or forsake him. Whoever looks after the need of his brother, God looks after his need; and whoever relieves a Muslim of distress, God will therefore relieve some of his distress on the day of resurrection. And whoever shields a Muslim, God will shield him on the day of resurrection."

Help on the Way

THE PROPHET said, "Whoever banishes one of the worries of the world from a believer, God banishes one of the worries of the day of resurrection from him.

"And whoever makes it easy for someone in distress, God makes it easy for him in the world and the hereafter.

"And God helps a devotee as long as the devotee helps his brother.

"And whoever follows a path seeking knowledge, God smoothes a path to Paradise for him.

"And whenever people gather in one of the houses of God, read the book of God, and study it together, peace descends upon them, and mercy envelops them, and angels surround them, and God mentions them to those around.

"And if someone's conduct slows him down, his lineage will not speed him on his way."

Appearance and Reality

THE MESSENGER OF GOD said, "There is one who is disheveled and dusty, turned away from doors, yet if he swears by God, God will fulfill it."

Men and Women

THE MESSENGER OF GOD said, "A believing man is not to hate a believing woman; if he dislikes one characteristic in her, he will like another one."

Faith and Character

THE MESSENGER OF GOD said, "The most perfect of believers in terms of faith is the most decent of them in terms of character. And the most decent of you are those who are best to their wives."

A Good Wife

THE MESSENGER OF GOD said, "The world is a provision, and the best of its provisions is a good wife."

Money Well Spent

THE MESSENGER OF GOD said, "There is the money you spend on the cause of God, and the money you spend to free the enslaved, and the money you donate to the poor, and the money you spend on your family: the greatest of these, in terms of reward, is what you spend on your family."

Friends and Neighbors

THE MESSENGER OF GOD said, "The best of friends, in the view of God Most High, is the one who is best to his friend. And the best of neighbors, in the view of God Most High, is the one who is best to his neighbors."

Glorification of God

THE MESSENGER OF GOD said, "Part of the glorification of God is respect for the elderly Muslim, and for one who knows the Qur'ān by heart without being fanatical about it or deviating from it; and respect for holders of authority who are just."

Young and Old

THE MESSENGER OF GOD said, "He is not one of us who does not treat our young with compassion or acknowledge the dignity of our elders."

The Influence of Association

THE PROPHET said, "A man inclines to the belief of his friend, so let each one of you watch out who he befriends."

The Shelter of God

THE PROPHET said, "There are seven whom God will shelter in divine shade on a day when there is no other shelter but God's: a just leader; a youth who grows up in the worship of God, the Great and Glorious; one whose heart is suspended in the mosques; two who love each other for the sake of God, meeting and parting for God's sake; a man who is seduced by a beautiful woman but says 'I fear God'; one who gives charity but conceals it so not even his left hand knows what his right hand gives; and one who remembers God in solitude and his eyes overflow."

Rendering Accounts

THE MESSENGER OF GOD said, "A mortal will remain standing until he is questioned about how he spent the years of his life, what he did with his knowledge, and where he earned his money and how he spent it; and how he wore out his body."

Earth's Stories

THE MESSENGER OF GOD recited, "On that day [the earth] will tell her stories . . ."

Then he said, "Do you know what her stories are?"

They said, "God and the Messenger know best."

He said, "Her stories are her testimonies about each mortal, male or female, what they did on the surface of the earth: she will say, 'You did such and such on such and such a day.' So these are her stories."

Repentance and Forgiveness

AMONG HIS ACCOUNTS of his Lord, the Prophet related, "A devotee sinned, then said, 'Oh, my God! Forgive me my sin!' "

And God said, "My servant has sinned, but realized he has a Lord who forgives sin and calls to account for sin."

Then he sinned again, and said, "Oh, my Lord! Forgive me my sin!"

And God said, "My servant has sinned, but realized he has a Lord who forgives sin and calls to account for sin."

Then he sinned again, and said, "Oh, my Lord! Forgive me my sin!"

And God said, "My servant has sinned, but realized he

has a Lord who forgives sin and calls to account for sin. I have forgiven my servant, so let him do what he wants."

(The words of God, "Let him do what he wants," mean that as long as he does thus and repents upon sinning, God will forgive him, for repentance demolishes what went before.)

Praise God

THE MESSENGER OF GOD said, "God is certainly pleased with a devotee who praises God for it when he eats a morsel, and praises God for it when it drinks a sip."

Initiation

ABŪ NAJIH AMR BIN ABASAH said, "When I was a heathen, I used to think the people were in error, and that they were unprincipled but worshipped idols. Then I heard of a man in Mecca relating new information. So I got on my camel and went to him."

I found the messenger of God keeping himself in concealment, his people besieging him. So I went to him secretly in Mecca and said to him, "What are you?"

He said, "I am a prophet."

I said, "And what is a prophet?"

He said, "God sent me."

I said, "And what did God send you for?"

He said, "For the joining of kin and the breaking of idols;

and that the unity of God be acknowledged, and nothing be associated therewith."

I said, "And who is with you in this?"

He said, "A freeman and a slave." In those days Abū Bakr and Bilāl were with him. May God be please with both of them."

I said, "I would follow you."

He said, "You cannot do it today. Don't you see my condition, and the state of my people? Rather, return to your people, and when you have heard that I have emerged, then come to me."

So I went to my people.

The Messenger of God arrived in Medina while I was with my people, and I began to inquire for news. And I inquired of people when they had been to Medina, until a party from my clan went to Medina and I said, "What is this man who has come to Medina doing?"

They said, "The people run to him, while his own tribe wanted him killed, though the heathens haven't been able to do that."

So I went to him in Medina and said, "Messenger of God, do you recognize me?"

He said, "Yes, you are the one who greeted me in Mecca."

Then I said, "Messenger of God, tell me what God has taught you, of which I am ignorant. Tell me about prayer."

He said, "Pray the morning prayer, then pray no more until the sun has risen the measure of a spear; for it comes into view when it rises between the horns of Satan, and the heathens bow to it at that time.

"Pray then, for prayer is witnessed and attended until the shadow shrinks to the size of the spear. Then desist from prayer, for it is then that Hell is fired up.

"Then when the shadow shifts direction, pray; for prayer is witnessed and attended until the afternoon prayer is said. Then desist from prayer until the sun sets, for it sets between the horns of Satan, and the heathen bow to it then."

Now I said to him, "Prophet of God, what about the ablution? Will you tell me about it?"

He said, "Whenever one sets about his ablutions and washes out his mouth and nose, the sins of his mouth and nose come out. Then when he washes his face, as instructed by God, the sins of his face come off from the borders of his whiskers with the water.

"Then one washes his hands up to the elbows, and the sins of his hands come off from his fingertips with the water.

"Then one wipes his head, and the sins of his head come off from the borders of his hair with the water.

"Then one washes his feet up to the ankles, and the sins of his feet come off from his toes with the water.

"Then when he stands and prays and praises God, and extols God, and glorifies God by what is worthy of God, and devotes his heart to God Most High, he departs from his sin as he was the day his mother bore him."

Dying

JĀBIR BIN ʿABDULLĀH relates that he heard the Prophet say three days before he died, "Let none of you die without a good opinion of God."

Forgiveness

THE MESSENGER OF GOD said, "God Most High said, 'O Son of Adam, as long as you call on Me and place your hope in Me, I forgive you what you have done, no matter how much. Son of Adam, even if your sins pile up to the clouds in the sky, if you then call on Me for forgiveness I will forgive you. Son of Adam, if you come to Me with an earth full of sins, yet you meet Me without associating anything with Me, I will come to you with that much forgiveness.' "

The World

THE MESSENGER OF GOD said, "The world is a prison for the believer, a paradise for the atheist."

Being in the World

THE MESSENGER OF GOD said, "Be in the world as if you were a stranger, or a wayfarer."

Reciprocity

A MAN came to the Prophet and said, "O Messenger of God, indicate to me an action whereby when I do so God loves me and people like me."

The Prophet said, "Be disinterested in the world, and God will love you. Be disinterested in what people have, and people will like you."

Greed

THE MESSENGER OF GOD said, "Two hungry wolves loose among sheep are not more harmful to them than the greed of a man for wealth and honor is to his religion."

Surplus and Sufficiency

THE MESSENGER OF GOD said, "O son of Adam, it is good for you to spend or give what is surplus, and bad for you to keep it. But you are not blamed for sufficiency, beginning with those for whom you are responsible."

Three Things

THE MESSENGER OF GOD said, "Three things I swear: I will tell you, so remember:

"One's wealth does not diminish by charity.

"No one who is wronged endures patiently but God increases his strength.

"No one begins begging but God introduces him to poverty."

Four Types of People

THE MESSENGER OF GOD said, "There are only four types in the world:

"A mortal whom God has given wealth and knowledge, and who is conscientious with them out of respect for his Sustainer, and unites his kin with them, and acknowledges God's right therein. This is the best state.

"A mortal whom God has given knowledge but not wealth, and who is sincere in intention, saying, 'If I had money, I would do what so-and-so does,' this being his resolve.

"The reward of these two is equivalent.

"Then there is the mortal whom God has given wealth but not knowledge, and who squanders his wealth without knowledge. He is not conscientious with it out of respect for his Sustainer, does not unite his kin with it, and does not acknowledge God's right to it. This is the worst state.

"Then there is the mortal whom God has given neither wealth nor knowledge, yet he says, 'If I had wealth, I would have done what so-and-so has done,' for that is his desire.

"The culpability of these two is equivalent."

Virtue and Sin

THE PROPHET said, "Virtue is goodness of character, and sin is what you devise in your self and hate for people to find out about it."

Humility in Practice

THE MESSENGER OF GOD said, "God has inspired me that you should be humble so that no one despises anyone, and no one oppresses anyone."

Arrogance and Vanity

THE PROPHET said, "Anyone with the slightest bit of arrogance in his heart will not enter Paradise."

Then a man said, "Surely a man likes his clothes and shoes to be nice."

The Prophet said, "Certainly God is beautiful and loves beauty. Arrogance is vain disregard of the real and contempt for people."

The Outcast

THE MESSENGER OF GOD said, "There are three to whom God will not speak on the day of resurrection, and whom God will not purify and will not regard; and there is a tremendous torment in store for them: an old man who fornicates, a ruler who deceives, and a man whose pride interferes with the support of his family."

Abodes in Paradise

THE MESSENGER OF GOD said, "I guarantee an abode on the edge of the garden of Paradise for whoever gives up disputation, even when in the right; and an abode in the middle of the Garden for whoever gives up telling untruths, even in jest; and an abode on the heights of the Garden for whoever is of good character."

Nearest and Furthest

THE MESSENGER OF GOD said, "Among those who are most dear to me, and who will be nearest to me on the day of resurrection, are those of you who are best in terms of character and morals. And those who are most despicable to me, and who will be furthest from me on the day of resurrection, are the prattlers, the braggarts, and the blow-hards."

People said, "Messenger of God, we know what prattlers and braggarts are, but what are blowhards?"

He said, "Those who are overbearing."

Kindness

THE MESSENGER OF GOD said, "God is kind, and loves kindness in all things."

He also said, "God is kind and loves kindness, and grants to kindness what is not granted to harshness, and what is not granted to anything else."

He also said, "Anything is beautified by inclusion of kindness, and marred by its lack."

People of Paradise

THE MESSENGER OF GOD said, "The people of Paradise are three: a just ruler who makes peace; a compassionate person who is tender-hearted toward all relatives and Muslims; and a decent person with dependents who is ashamed to be importunate."

Leaders

THE MESSENGER OF GOD said, "The best of your leaders are those whom you love and who love you, and whom you pray for and who pray for you. And the worst of your leaders are those whom you hate and who hate you, and whom you curse and who curse you."

The Just

THE MESSENGER OF GOD said, "The just will be on plat-forms of light in the presence of God; those who are just in their decisions, with their families, and with what they are in charge of."